Confessions of a Troubled *Christian Pilgrim*

Reflections on
Difficult Questions
for Contemporary
Christians

Robert Chancellor

WESTBOW
P R E S S®
A DIVISION OF THOMAS NELSON
& ZONDERVAN

WestBow Press books may be ordered through booksellers or by contacting:

WestBow Press
A Division of Thomas Nelson & Zondervan
1663 Liberty Drive
Bloomington, IN 47403
www.westbowpress.com
844-714-3454

ISBN: 978-1-6642-0343-3 (sc)
ISBN: 978-1-6642-0345-7 (hc)
ISBN: 978-1-6642-0344-0 (e)

Library of Congress Control Number: 2020916292

Print information available on the last page.

WestBow Press rev. date: 09/08/2020

Dedicated to my wife, who encouraged me to dream again; to my parents, who never gave up on me; and to a Christian counselor who believed in my writing.

Contents

Preface

I thought about writing a book for a long time. I discussed it with my counselor, and he thought that this was the right time for me to put together a book. The one thing I have right now is the gift of time. My wife and I adopted a troubled child, and we are beset with many problems. I have many questions, questions of a spiritual nature. As an American and as a Christian in my late fifties, I have contemplated what my Christian faith stands for but more importantly where Christianity stands in the world and particularly America.

I graduated from the seminary in the late 1980s with a master of divinity. I had dreams of a church, a marriage, and children. As a Hoosier by heritage and someone who values family, the image of my future was shaped by the expectations of my own background. Yet here I am, with a troubled present and a broken past. The older we get, the faster time seems to pass us by. This reminds me of a piece of wisdom shared with me from a wise farm lady in Indiana, who explained how the mystery of time works. She said, "Robert, the days are long, but the years are short."

I sometimes wonder, where did those years go and my dreams with them? What became of my Jerusalem? Why do I find myself struggling to sing the Lord's song in a foreign land? I suspect that many of you are asking the same question.

My book takes you on a journey into this critical question. So many books are written with a formula for how to become a successful person or a better Christian. These books are written by famous people to tout their accomplishments and to encourage you to follow their example. That's not the purpose of this book.

I want to share with you what I learned from failure, pain, and frustration, what I learned from disappointment. I trust that what I learned from my journey in this foreign land will open insights into your own journey. I look at my life and beliefs through the lens of the New Testament; I see the spiritual poverty of contemporary American culture.

How are we to understand the Christian journey? A wise person once said, "A trip of a thousand miles begins with a single step." That's how I view this book and how you should view your own journey. What I really want to do is to offer you food for thought, a framework in which to understand the journey we are on and hopefully continue that journey to its ultimate end.

Introduction

Why did I write this book? It was a question that I had pondered for a few days before embarking on this project. My wife believed it was time for me to share what was in my heart and soul. Honestly, I have been writing this book for several years now in terms of the thoughts I've shared in term papers, articles, sermons, and blogs, and in my private journaling.

However, I decided it was time to bring these thoughts together into one book. Late in life, Anna Mary Robertson Moses, better known as "Grandma Moses," found her one gift in primitive art paintings depicting real life. Recently, I came to a similar conclusion. I have only one profoundly important thing to share with the world, and that is my thoughts. I can paint these pictures of truth with my words. This book is my work of art.

My faith and life have been on a peculiar trajectory, with twists and turns that have uniquely formed our perspective on God, religion, and culture. I grew up in three states and have been affiliated with seven Christian denominations, attended an evangelical seminary, and served in three Methodist churches in the South and congregations with my home denomination in Florida and Indiana. I am also the adoptive father of a teenager. I am involved in mental health advocacy, but I will share more about that later.

I am one of four children. My two older siblings were born in Indiana; my younger brother and I were born in Tennessee, and I spent my teenage years in South Florida. My father was a scientist and executive in pharmaceuticals, with several patents in his name. My mother is a journalist, poet, composer, and actress.

I hope that the story of my journey will provide hope and comfort to those who are seeking faith but may be troubled by the contradictory and hypocritical messages they've gotten from organized religion. Let me say from the outset that I am a firm believer in Christ, and I believe in the value of the church.

However, I am aware that our institutions of faith and their representatives are human. After all, I attended such institutions and served them as a representative. Part of my confession as a Christian pilgrim is that I learned as much from introspection about my own failures as I did from observing others.

After all, Christ is closest to us not when we are brimming with pride and self-confidence but when we are broken and vulnerable; we must be open to learning from our failures. As you read about my journey, my prayer for you is that you'll see that your own journey has value. Your disillusionment need not lead to despair and cynicism, but instead to a deeper and more abiding faith. Let us begin.

Shall We Begin?

Wherever you are on your journey, I want you to know that God is ready to meet you. How do I know this? I learned it the hard way. Jesus promised that "my yoke is easy, and my burden is light" (Matthew 11:30 ESV). God is not in the business of making it complicated to find him. He understands the complexity of our life and does everything conceivable to make access to him simple. In 1 John 4:8 (ESV), we read "God is love," which means that God defines for us what *love* means and not the other way around.

God defines for us what love means, what it looks like, and how it behaves. Love looks like Jesus. It acts like Jesus. It is tender like Jesus. It sacrifices like Jesus. Sometimes, it is even stern like Jesus. On rare occasions, it speaks eloquently like Jesus. Such love encompasses emotions, but it is larger than that, and it is reflected more in action than it is in feeling.

Why start here? Because Paul taught that in our Christian journey, we don't merely plod along but are in a kind of race. He used this metaphor in 1 Corinthians 9. Paul spoke of the Christian pilgrimage in terms of learning to rely on Christ more deeply, identifying with Christ more deeply, and finally becoming like Christ more deeply. These three goals constitute the main goal of the Christian pilgrimage.

Sounds simple, right? Beware. The simplicity of these goals belies the personal cost involved in reaching them.

Any goal that runs up against the grain of our selfishness, our thoughtlessness, our ego, and our hang-ups is going to require a lot of prayer and work. Like a great sculptor, God wants to take the raw piece of marble that is us and chip away at it until the masterpiece that he wants to create out of us emerges. Sculpting is a process of work and patience. One can only speculate about the time it took for the great Michelangelo to create his glorious statues out of carved marble and rock. What Christ makes of us will be his work in us.

Unlike the inanimate rock of a Michelangelo masterpiece, God requires our cooperation in allowing him to carve us into the image of Christ. He sometimes allows situations to happen in our lives to get us back to a place where he can continue to work on us. He provides us with comfort in the hard places, but his long-term goal is to develop our character into Christlikeness.

Some parts of our marble are more resistant and require hard, painful, and deep chiseling. At those moments, we might want to run from what God is doing in our lives. Experiences that lead to growth can be painful and even heartbreaking. We would not choose them. In fact, it is only in hindsight that I look back at events in my life with a sense of thankfulness. I certainly didn't feel that way when they occurred. Admittedly, I felt more anger at God than thankfulness. Yet as a sign that hangs on my wall states, "Trouble is what God uses to mold us for better things."

Upon later reflection, I realized a still more important truth. We often unfairly blame God for our decisions, even those we never consulted him on. After all, Galatians 6:7 (RSV) reads, "Whatsoever a man sows, that he will also reap." Many people blame God for circumstances they engineered without any regard to what the Lord wanted for them. Hopefully, as we grow in our faith, we more often seek God's guidance for difficult decisions. I hope my book offers some helpful perspective along those lines.

God bless you.

Chapter 1

REFLECTIONS ON RELIGION, FAITH, AND SALVATION

Is There a Difference between Religion and Faith?

We all need the church, but the church has become adept at offering things people are not asking for and being oblivious to what people need. We are looking for connection, but we are offered membership. We are looking for fellowship, but we are given a committee to serve on. We are looking for shepherds to nurture us, but we often encounter power brokers who bully us instead. We are looking to have our questions taken seriously, but we are told to have faith, give our money, and attend church regularly.

Faith and religion are related but not synonymous, contrary to popular belief. Religion constitutes established beliefs, sacred traditions, and church institutions. Faith, on the other hand, is a connection to a mysterious reality that is demonstrated in trust and obedience. The failure to distinguish between these two concepts creates confusion in the mind of the average spiritual seeker. Unfortunately, in our common understanding, faith is defined as accepting a set of beliefs, observing a set of practices, and exhibiting an institutional loyalty. This, of course, is wrong.

The marketplace of Christian denominations can create confusion in the mind and soul of the average person. This confusion is highlighted by the competing faith claims of diverse groups. Faith becomes a product of prepackaged beliefs and practices, and closing the sale becomes the objective for new converts (or customers). On the other hand, faith is more than just sincere believing. The object of faith also matters.

My wife and I used to joke that I was becoming a minister in the Church of the Glowing Pickle. The kind of church where people can just feel good about believing in something, or anything, for that matter. Faith without a valid object can be delusional believing. But when belief meets the real God revealed in Jesus, it becomes genuine faith. Yet much of what people get caught up in is a cultural belief of religious tradition instead of a spiritual faith. Or as some say, "It's about a relationship with God." Religion forms the framework and knob of the door. But only faith can turn the knob and open the door to the reality of the living God.

When you ask people about their faith, some devout souls will say, "Methodist bred and Methodist dead," or "I am a loyal Catholic [Presbyterian, Congregationalist, or Baptist]." Those traditions were an important part of my spiritual journey as a Christian and enriched the scope of my Christian faith. Yet none of them exclusively defines my faith for me.

My faith is a connection with God through his Son Jesus, and it is deepened by my association with other Christians, but my faith also stands apart as a spiritual mystery. True Christian Catholicism acknowledges that no matter how the visible church may be partitioned by the preferences of human beings, it is Jesus who creates the reality of the invisible church. Fellowship is determined more authentically by the presence of the Holy Spirit than by the imposition of an organization.

The work of the Lord requires a channel and an organization. So denominations are needed to serve the Kingdom of God, and to instruct, guide, and encourage Christians in the faith. Denominations, at their best, can offer to Christians a substantial sense of belonging and a concrete channel of mission, giving, service, and worship. Denominations, and their structures, can be excellent servants in God's Kingdom.

Unfortunately, these institutions can also become troubling idols. Many founders of church bodies were more reformers and pragmatists than institution builders. Martin Luther intended to reform the existing church, not start a new one. John Wesley sought to create a movement within Anglicanism and not create a new church body.

For instance, one particular denomination took the pragmatic methods of John Wesley, which were innovative and creative for his time, to reach their masses by hardening his imaginative and flexible methodology into an unimaginative and unbending ideology. Its official rule book became its Bible. The ecclesiastical structure became its idol.

As a connectional church, pastors would be appointed by officers of the denomination, rather than called by the churches in the context of its regional bodies. Pastors of small churches and charges would frequently be moved around and reappointed by its officers on a yearly basis.

Yet I noticed in this denomination, the larger, wealthier parishes enjoyed long pastoral tenures. This system that extolled the virtues of an itinerant or travelling ministry showed political favoritism toward money and influence, despite the fact that every expert church study out there had argued in favor of long pastoral tenures as the key to church growth and health.

This undercut the pragmatic and practical legacy of John Wesley himself and hurt the prospects of smaller churches ever growing larger. I daresay if Wesley were alive today, he would argue for scrapping the itinerant ministry in favor of promoting long tenures in all the churches, but that's just my troubled opinion.

I once commented about this situation to a pastor friend of mine, who remarked, "Robert, there is no fighting the system."

The system was the idol and we were all to pay homage to it; all other values were to be sacrificed, all other considerations set aside, and no negotiation was possible without the blessing of its high priests. Thus, it had become like the church that Wesley had wanted to change, only worse.

To be sure, this church was exceptionally successful in America and around the world, due to its impressive organization. But like many movements, it could confuse some by equating the structures of religion with the mystery of faith itself. Across the board of denominational life, idolatry has been one of Christianity's biggest problems, in the opinion of this Christian pilgrim.

This reality has turned off many people new to the faith, people who were required to acknowledge and pay homage to the peculiar practices of local church congregations and to the power brokers of established church bodies, some of whom could be abusive with their power, hardly modelling the example of the good shepherd that the church is supposed to point us toward.

Some in church life seem unable to distinguish between authority and authoritarianism. Authority, like the authority of our Lord Jesus, is grounded in evoking respect for one's calling, integrity, and compassion. Authoritarianism, like the leadership of the Pharisees and temple priests, is rooted primarily in power. This constitutes the difference between shepherds and ecclesiastical bullies.

Note to the reader: There are many fine people in the groups associated with the legacies of John Wesley and Martin Luther. I have known and loved many of them. I attended a Methodist church for a few years, and one year, I had what's called a three-point charge, where I served as pastor to three churches, also known as a circuit. The early Methodist pastors who served such churches were called circuit riders.

I also teamed up with a Lutheran pastor in Florida to do ecumenical projects, and I travelled with him and several other Lutherans, including a bishop, to Israel and Rome. So my criticisms are not blanket indictments but based on personal experience, knowledge, and affection.

The postmodern and denominational era is ending the custom

of denominational identity and the traditions association with church bodies. Churches are increasingly distancing themselves from their denominational identities and naming themselves according to their own sense of mission. Churches with titles like "the church of divine fellowship," or "the healing waters," or "the church of the funky savior," for that matter, are becoming the trend.

Some aspects of this trend are quite encouraging. The formerly overbearing, and at times idolatrous, ecclesiastical structures are becoming more servant-like in assisting the mission and purpose of local churches. However, a new problem has emerged, where images and experiences are becoming more prominent than actual biblical instruction.

There is nothing inherently wrong with images. The early church communicated with images like fish, the shepherd's staff, anchors, circles, and combinations of these images into Chrismon's and other symbols. Unfortunately, it troubles me as a Christian pilgrim that substance has started to take a back seat to image and experience. Contemporary Christianity runs the risk of turning into the Church of the Glowing Pickle by undercutting why sound knowledge of the object of our worship matters, in terms of promoting an authentic biblical faith.

A balance between an authentic faith and a wholesome church structure, while difficult to maintain, is a healthy pursuit for a church that Christ called to make disciples for himself and to minister in his name.

The Meaning of Christian Conversion

In the winter of 1987, I was assisting with a mission and ministry conference at my seminary. I was working with a student I had developed a decent rapport with, or so I thought. We stopped briefly for a lunch after a long morning of setting up booths and coordinating projects. This student asked me, "How did you come to know the Lord?" I was only too happy to share my story. But after I shared it, instead of looking inspired or shedding tears, he looked at me like I had just told him I used crystal meth as a child.

Why the negative reaction? Well, my story did not fit a popular Christian narrative about conversion. My story was different. First, I had many Christian influences from a noticeably young age. I had a grandmother who visited us a whole month out of every year, and she talked about her faith in Jesus frequently. I had Christian parents, and my dad insisted that we all go to church. In short, I was familiar with the story of Jesus. I occasionally even read from the Bible and was familiar with some of the stories in it from Sunday school.

In April 1975, we had a new interim minister at our United Presbyterian Church in South Florida. My mom liked the former minister much better, but the new minister, a very distinguished graduate from Union Seminary in Richmond, Virginia, was our solid stand-in. That Sunday was like most we had attended. I was daydreaming about robots and rockets, like I usually did.

There was a unique architectural feature to this A-frame-shaped church. The front top of the sanctuary had several skylights, which allowed sunshine to pour through over a large metal cross attached to the back wall. Our minister was droning on, as he usually did, about some important social topic in the world, as it related to the message of Jesus. I do not recall a word he uttered and have no remembrance of what hymns we sang. I just started, for no reason, to look at that cross, with the rays coming down it from the lovely skylights.

Then something odd began to stir in me emotionally. I started to feel some actual warmth coming off that cross, like something was being communicated to me. I could not hear anything, but a phrase kept repeating in my mind: *Robert, it is true. It is all true. Jesus is not only real. He not only loves the world. He also loves you. It is true. It is true. It is true.* Well, by the end of the service, my parents and siblings were concerned about my emotional state. They thought something had upset me during the service.

So my dad asked me what was wrong.

I was crying and said, "Daaaad ... it is true; it is true. Jesus is real, and I believe in him."

Dad then took me up to the pastor, who was greeting people going out the front door, and I said to the pastor, "I ... I ... believe in Jesus. I know it is true. He is true."

Our minister, who looked a bit nervous and perturbed by the whole spectacle, shook my hands and said curtly, "That is very nice, young man; I think."

He had no idea how to respond to what I had just experienced. After I went home, I went into our back yard and took two pieces of wood I had found in our garage and nailed them together. My father helped me put that cross up on the wall of my room. It was then that both of my parents thought that the ministry might be my calling.

I thought it was a pretty neat story, not one to inspire contempt, anyway. However, being at a non-mainline institution, my story just did not fit in. The denomination of my seminary was influenced by the revival tradition of Christianity. These Christians were used to hearing stories of lost souls who came to the light after hearing a sermon about the fires of hell or the joys of heaven, followed up by songs like "Just as I Am," usually with the respondent finally coming to the altar after the fourth stanza.

Their idea of reaching people reminded me of the great and cheery sermons by eighteenth-century preacher Jonathan Edwards, called "Sinners in the Hands of an Angry God," whereby Edwards describes sinners as being like spiders dangling on a thin web over an all-consuming fire, designed to torment them for all of eternity.[1] How could I think about heaven apart from being frightened about the destiny of my soul? Yet what happens when those who are steeped in that tradition of Christian conversion come across a story like mine? Some will doubt that I was saved.

Therein lies the problem. I'm open to different methods of reaching people, from the praying rooms of Finney, to the altar calls of Moody, to the four spiritual laws of Bill Bright and Campus

Crusade for Christ, to evangelism explosion of D. James Kennedy and its various imitations. Yet we forget that some are raised into the faith like young Timothy:

> I am reminded of your sincere faith, which first lived in your grandmother Lois, and in your mother Eunice and, I am persuaded, now lives in you also. (2 Timothy 1:5 NIV)

The Holy Spirit is the one who brings hearts to a conviction about Christ.

> And when he comes, he will convict the world of its sin, and of God's righteousness, and of the coming judgment. (John 16:8 NLT)

Let's apply the standard methods of outreach to the conversion story of Paul (or Saul). What happened on the road to Damascus? Did Jesus come in a vision and say, "Saul, it's time for you to come to the altar and confess your sins"? Did Jesus implore Saul to pray about the state of his soul? Did Jesus tell Saul that he had a wonderful plan for his life and there was this chasm that could only be bridged by faith? Lastly, did Jesus say to Saul, "If I were to ask you why I should let you into heaven, what you would you say?" Truthfully, none of those methods were employed by the Lord in Paul's conversion.

Paul, otherwise known as Saul, was knocked off his horse, and he asked who Jesus was; he says, "Here I am, Saul. I am Jesus. I am not asking you to believe anything. I am telling you I am real, and I am angry that you are persecuting Me and the church. Frankly, I have been trying to reach you for a long time, but you are just too stubborn to take a hint, which is why you are kicking against the goads." Saul is blinded by Jesus so that Ananias can take care of him, and Jesus shows Ananias in a vision that Saul is going to suffer a lot, and he has no choice in the matter.

Many speak of Pauline conversions, but Paul's conversion contradicts much of what Christians steeped in the revival tradition believe about conversions. We are talking about a person who hated Jesus, hated his followers and wanted to destroy them, and then against his will, he's told he is going to serve Jesus, help his followers, and promote his message.

Finally, at the tail end of his conversion story, he begins to like the idea that he is the servant of Jesus; after his conversion takes place, he feels convicted by how terrible he was. In short, his story is the reverse of how many understand the conversion process is supposed to happen. After all, we are supposed to feel guilt, then respond to our call, have an emotional catharsis, and then feel relieved that we are now saved. Paul got saved, had an emotional catharsis, responded to his call, and then started to feel guilt. Get the idea?

Well, you could argue that Paul was a notable exception to the established rule. Yes, you could, but the point here is this: Jesus and the Holy Spirit can use any method, circumstance, or people to influence someone into embracing the Kingdom of God. A famous example of this is when Christian writer C. S. Lewis decided, at the age of thirty-two, that he was going to believe in Jesus, while riding in the sidecar of his brother's motorcycle. This conversion happened soon after having a conversation with J. R. R. Tolkien, who was trying to convince Lewis that "Jesus was the true myth."[2]

I recently read about some interesting stories of Muslims converting to Christianity; in many respects, their conversion testimonies parallel that of Paul. There are reports of Muslim Christian converts who see visions of Jesus telling them they need to follow him. It is a remarkable and largely underreported work of the Holy Spirit that is currently going in the world.[3]

As for me, various people in my life planted seeds that did not bloom until later. Even D. L. Moody was influenced by his Sunday school teacher, Richard Kimball. Paul was "kicking against the goads," so perhaps God was using people and circumstances to knock at the door of his heart. Gamaliel, his rabbinic teacher, wisely warned Paul not to persecute the Christians because he might find himself fighting God.[4]

Rarely is any of this instantaneous, but there is no right way or wrong way for it to all come to fruition. It can happen at a camp meeting, a revival, a mass evangelistic rally like Billy Graham used to hold, or a one-on-one discussion about Jesus; it can occur from a friendship with a Christian or in a Sunday school class; or it can be a bolt out of the blue at a very mundane worship service, like it happened to me. It can even involve someone getting knocked off their horse in the desert and blinded, as it happened to Paul.

In short, conversion is a mystery that involves the Holy Spirit and the Spirit's involvement in and influence on a single, solitary life. Just because someone's testimony of grace doesn't parallel our own doesn't mean that it should be dismissed, like mine was by that student who I thought was my friend. I never dismissed how the Holy Spirit had functioned in his life, or that of other students at my seminary, for that matter, but it troubled me and even hurt me that my testimony was not acceptable.

Are there dubious testimonies of grace and conversion? Yes, but more likely than not, the disingenuous stories reflect the narrative that many Christians will most readily buy into and not question, as I see it. This has always troubled me.

I have even heard what amounts to conversion experiences (or least renewal experiences) from movements like Cursillo (a Roman Catholic movement) or the Walk to Emmaus (a Protestant renewal and conversion program modelled after Cursillo).[5] I am not inclined to question how a person comes to Christ, because look at my story. I am more inclined to be sensitive to their attitudes and Christian actions or "fruits" that reflect how Jesus is present in them.

While I value testimonies of personal awakenings, I was also troubled by Christians who center their whole testimony on the event of their conversion. When I worked at various jobs as a Kelly temp in Virginia, I heard many stories of "how I got saved." In short, their primary testimonies were about what happened to them, instead of how God changed the direction of their life journey.

The direction of my life journey was forever altered by a change in me. Paul's life journey was forever altered by what happened to him. This could be said of preachers, missionaries, doctors, and others. If all that happened was a transaction involving belief in Jesus to be spared eternal torment, then what kind of conversion took place? What kind of change in life trajectory occurred? In my view, at least from my understanding of the Gospels, the call to follow Jesus is part of the conversion deal.

I don't like to judge or to be judged. However, many parables of Jesus, from the "wheat and the tares" and "the sheep and the goats" to the Last Judgment, all indicate the basic truth that not all who confess the name of Jesus are going to be sincere.

If there is a conversion test, the most valid one is in terms of the kind of life that is produced. This appears to be the test that Jesus himself presented to us. Matthew 7:20 (NASB) says, "So then, you will know them by their fruits." I cannot read another person's heart. I cannot always even read my own. However, I can see what others do or act and affirm or not affirm based on that. This reminds me of what a Sunday school teacher once shared with me: "I cannot judge anyone's heart, but I am a fruit inspector."

Christ calls us to a journey where he is the center. If he is not, then those who profess their conversion should ask themselves why he is not (or at least they should be challenged by others with that question). As Paul himself said, we are to work out our salvation "with fear and trembling" (Philippians 2:12 NIV). May the reader find an authentic faith and awareness of Jesus Christ.

On Being Good

I was a religious kid. I enjoyed reading my Bible, talking about Jesus, and contemplating spiritual things. Did this get on my siblings' nerves? Are you kidding? Sometimes, I think God gives us siblings to teach us humility. I know mine did. My brother would occasionally tease me with the words "You're just so good." Yet, to be honest, many equate being Christian with being good. They perceive the Christian life as one opportunity after another to show just how good they are. After all, we need to honor Christ by our actions, don't we?

Far be it from me to criticize the idea of wanting to be good, although to be honest, I know some Christians who are insufferable in their compulsion to show you just how good they are. So the question really boils down to this: Am I good? I think I'm okay. I've never robbed a 7/11, and I try to be nice and compassionate to older people, children, and animals.

Yet to be good in the sense that God is good takes the idea to an entirely different level. When we lived in the New York area, my wife and I occasionally took a train into Manhattan. We changed trains in Secaucus, New Jersey, where we frequently saw a Hassidic Jewish family at the station.

The gentleman was exceptionally dignified and religiously garbed, and his adoring wife was groomed to the hilt. The children were well-dressed and exceptionally well-behaved. In fact, there was nothing about that picture I could really criticize, and here I was with my worn-out T-shirt and jeans, and not always great disposition. Could I claim to be as good as this gentleman and his family?

Many things began to percolate in my spirit as I reflected on this. Didn't Jesus say our righteousness had to exceed that of the scribes and Pharisees in order to see the Kingdom of God? As he said in Matthew 5:48 (NIV), "So be perfect, as your heavenly father is perfect," which Martin Luther described as "the Counsel of Despair."[6]

Yet Paul said in Romans 7:18 (KJV), "For I know that in me [that is, in my flesh] nothing good dwells." If we are to take Paul's counsel here at face value, then there is nothing good, in the ultimate sense, in my natural human state to draw upon. Our life itself is a paradox, a paradox of two conflicting states of being. We find ourselves drawn into a conflict between two contradictory impulses. One impulse is our desire to serve God, and the other impulse is our basic human nature, which is preoccupied with more selfish concerns.

I don't know about you, but I've had dreams where I was able to fly like Superman, only to awaken and discover that I remained earthbound due to a force called gravity. Reaching for goodness is like jumping up, with the hopes of reaching the sky, only to come plopping down after getting three feet off the ground. However, we can be carried aloft into the stratosphere by the power of a jet airplane, a power much greater than ourselves. We read further in Romans:

> For I have the desire to do what is good, but I cannot carry out. For I do not do the good I want to do, but the evil I do not want to do—this I keep on doing. Now if I do what I do not want to do, it is no longer I who do it, but it is sin living in me that does it. So, I find this law at work: Although I want to do good, evil is right there with me. For in my inner being I delight in God's law; but I see another law at work within me. What a wretched man I am! Who will rescue me from this body that is subject to death? Thanks be to God, who delivers me through Jesus Christ our Lord! (Romans 7:18–28 NIV)

How is goodness even possible for you or me? This seems like an impossible achievement, but perhaps it's possible, as a gift of deliverance. This is not a goodness we achieve but a goodness we receive. I am not a Christian because I am good; I am a Christian because Jesus Christ is good. There is after all a fundamental difference between these two propositions, is there not? One proposition makes me and my efforts to be good the center of my faith; the other focuses on Jesus Christ and his work of goodness in me.

No one exemplified the paradox of spiritual goodness better than Paul himself. Paul had an undeniable dark side. He began his life being willing to persecute, torture, and imprison others in the name of his Jewish faith. Even after his conversion, the New Testament strongly suggests that he could be abrasive and unkind toward Jesus's followers (and misogynistic, to boot). This is why many Christians today have an issue with Paul.

Yet Paul wrote many of the most beautiful and heartfelt words in the New Testament. How does one account for the discrepancy? Like us, he was a person of light and darkness, but over time, he came to trust in the light of God's grace alone, to lift him out of his darkness, to new heights of love and humility.

We can also thus be lifted. In fact, by my own efforts, I will never be as good as that Hassidic gentlemen in Secaucus, much less a scribe or a Pharisee. Yet by grace, our life can reflect a goodness that exceeds them. I'm never going to be perfect, either, in the sense that Christ is perfect, and the good news is that I don't have to be. In fact, perfect goodness, perfect love, and perfect righteousness are already here in the Holy Spirit, who brings us into the presence of Christ.

This goodness can flow through us as a gift. We can be a channel of this goodness. I love the way Paul expresses it in 2 Corinthians 4:7 (BSB): "Now we have this treasure [meaning the love and grace of Christ] in jars of clay or earthen vessels [meaning the broken and imperfect vessel of our bodies] to show that this surpassingly great power is from God and not from us." Through faith, Christ rescues the vessel of our bodies and souls. Therefore, we can open the vessels of our bodies to be a cup that Christ can pour himself into and pour himself out of. We read in 2 Peter, "His divine power has given us everything required for life and godliness through the knowledge of him who called us by his own glory and goodness" (2 Peter 1:3 CSB).

You and I can be receptacles of the perfection of Christ. It is not an achievement; it has nothing to do with our goodness and everything to do with the power and goodness of Jesus Christ. By faith, we can claim this goodness as Christ's gift to us.

Restoring a Proper New Testament Respect for Divine Mystery in Redemption and Salvation

Some people fail to reckon with many paradoxes in the New Testament and in biblical faith because they require trusting God way too much. Sometimes, we love our theological formulas more than we love the Lord. We have the "Plan of Salvation," the "Romans Road," and other various programs. Am I against theological formulas? No. They help us to understand and define many important truths. They also make for excellent evangelistic tools.[7]

Yet truth is often paradoxical. Paul says, "When I am weak, then I am strong" (2 Corinthians 12:10 NIV). We have three distinct persons in our Trinity, and yet we are told they constitute one divine being. We are free yet elected. We can feel sure that we are called, but it is God who separates the wheat from the chaff and the sheep from the goats.

When I attended community college in Florida, I had a humanities professor who ridiculed idea that the Lord could make contradictory ideas possible. "Could God make a square circle?" he retorted. I wish I knew what I know now. As I shared in my last section, two seemingly contradictory ideas that both appear to be true are called a *paradox*. Many of the greatest truths ever contemplated were paradoxes. The idea that God could be three persons and yet one divine being is just such a paradox, in this case $1 + 1 + 1 = 1$ or $3 = 1$. In fact, many see mystery in the New Testament as another word for paradox.

The conflict between Calvinism and Arminianism occurred because of a failure on both sides to reckon with mystery and paradox. A desire to nail the purpose of God down to a linear formula that only serves to widen the gap between those who assert we are free to believe or not and those who believe we are powerless in matters of election and salvation.

Reformed theology asserts that faith is a result, a sign, or a fruit of salvation since it is God alone who elects us to salvation.

Wesleyan Arminian theology (of Jacob Arminius), or free will theology, asserts that faith is a cause of salvation, but God enables the exercise of will or faith through a common or prevenient grace.[8] Yet if God can choose us to be Christians for salvation, could he also choose non-Christians for redemption as well, or at least those who never openly professed a faith in Jesus? After all, according to Reformed theology, faith is a result and not a cause of election. Therefore, how are we to know who all the elect is? Could there be more elect than professing Christians?

What if neither position is entirely wrong or entirely right, but each side merely reflects one side of a deeper paradox that Paul and other apostles tried to express as finite and limited human beings? What is the chief sin that those of faith are constantly chided about in the New Testament? Is it not the sin of presumption?

Presumption is defined as an idea that is assumed to be true but is not known to be true for certain, but is often used as the basis of other ideas. Presumption is also defined as a kind of arrogance and disrespect. We are told in scripture to be aware of signs of the times about apocalyptic matters, and yet we are also told that only the Father and not even the Son knows the day or the hour when the Son of Man will return to the earth. We are to be aware of spiritual realities but not assume that we understand everything about them or that we always follow or understand God's purpose.

However, we see this presumption in the charts of John Hagee and Hal Lindsey as if to say, "God, this is the plan you are to follow. We are your self-appointed prophets; listen carefully."[9] We see this in the words of Jesus, who speaks of an arrogant and presumptuous follower:

> Not everyone who says to me, Lord, Lord, will enter the Kingdom of heaven, but only the one who does the will of my father who is in heaven. Many will say to me on that day, Lord, Lord, did we not prophesy in your name and in your name drive out demons and, in your name, perform many

miracles? Then I tell them plainly, I never knew you. Away from me, you evil doers! (Matthew 7:21–23 NIV)

We find presumption in the positions of both Christian exclusivism and universalism, or inclusivism, as some call it. One is generally held by conservative Christians and the other by liberal Christians. Yet both are equally presumptuous, it seems to me. Both make assumptions about the will of God.

The exclusivist presumes that by God's nature and covenant, he must only save those who have professed a faith in Jesus and condemn the rest. The universalist or inclusivist presumes that God's election must include all, and it would be contrary to love for anyone to be excluded from salvation. One shortchanges God's mercy, and the other challenges his judgment or disputes the idea that he has the right to exclude anyone. Neither position, in my view, fully comes to terms with the paradoxes present in New Testament teaching, and both positions end up doing damage to our view of God's character.[10]

When I was in seminary, the school was deeply embroiled in a theological controversy over inerrancy and its implications for Christian theology. Students were arguing over whether we would have blood on our hands if we didn't do everything we could to share the salvation message of Jesus with others. In my systematic theology class, the instructor said something I will never forget (every now and then, even a theology professor will say something worthwhile). He said, "In the economy of God, there may be other possibilities, but for the Christian, there are no other assurances."[11]

Over the past thirty years, I've thought long and hard about that statement. There is enough in those words to make both my liberal and conservative Christian friends cringe. God has obligated himself to the covenant he made at the Cross to save those who believe in his Son. Yet what about those who never hear the good news or are leaning toward faith but never quite make the confession before death? Would God consider having mercy on those in other faiths? Could there be more elect in the world than the number of professing Christians?

Is this an argument for universalism? No. It is an argument, I believe, for the sovereignty and freedom of God. The Lord can act independent of his covenant obligations based on the council of his own will. This is no guarantee of all going to heaven or of none going to hell. However, I believe that I possess one thing as a Christian that non-Christians don't have, and that is an assurance of salvation. This assurance reflects the covenant the Father established through Jesus Christ.

I find this conviction to be a helpful bridge between Universalism, Arminianism, and Calvinistic exclusivism. Each position can find support in scripture, but none of these positions adequately addresses the objection of the other or reconciles contrasting biblical statements. Universalism is an old theme in Christian theology and can be found in Origen, one of the church fathers. Karl Barth, the premier neoorthodox and reformed theologian of the twentieth century, argued that all are elected in Christ. Yet I still believe that only through faith can any of us know that our eternal life will be in the presence of the Lord.[12] It also seems to me that whether faith is a cause in the Arminian sense or a result in the Calvinistic sense, or all are elected in a Universalistic sense, faith is still something that needs to be evoked by the proclamation of the Word and the convicting work of the Spirit. There is ample biblical support for that contention.

My calling as a Christian is therefore to proclaim the hope that I know in Jesus as a certain assurance of faith. My calling is not to the judge the world, condemn the world, or decide who God should send to hell. I might have some opinions about that, but the Lord is much better qualified than I am to make that judgment, and because I have confidence in his character; I know that his judgments will be right. Therefore, I am willing to concede that the Supreme Being of the universe might possess some discretion in his dealings with his creatures; he certainly has a divine right to such a prerogative.

Besides, while I love to share the assurance that comes with Jesus, I think it's cruel to deny anyone the possibility of hope; that includes both the living and the dead. Should God hold someone's ignorance against them? Will he judge their failure to fully profess their faith before they die? Putting this idea in a different way, God is inclusive in his potential redemption of others, but he exclusively offers assurance only to those who place their faith in Jesus.

Something that's often overlooked in the discussion on election is the eternal nature of God himself. The entire Bible points to his nonlinear and timeless nature. He refers to himself as "I AM" over three hundred times, from Genesis through Revelation. God disclosed to Abraham and others in ancient times his timeless nature and did so in an amazingly simple but profound way. God's self-description spoke volumes about his actual nature. He never describes himself as the "Great I WAS" or the "Great I WILL BE." God is always the "Great I AM." I think that is incredibly significant.[13]

In Revelation 22:13 (KJV), God is described as the "Alpha and Omega, the beginning and the end." As linear creatures traveling down the river of time, we all have a beginning, a middle, and an end, but not God. Linear space-time is a construct of creation and not the ultimate reality. Nonlinear eternity is. This is the realm in which God exists, apparently.

What does this suggest? That the rules of time do not apply to God but only to the reality where we exist. In John 8:58 (KJV), we read "before Abraham was, I AM." We read in Revelation 13:8 (KJV), "He was slain from the foundation of the world." This passage suggests that the Lord was present for both Creation and the Crucifixion, at the same time. It could be argued that God exists everywhere in time simultaneously, because he is not limited by the rules of space-time.

There is no past or future with God but only an eternal present. This has significant implications for the doctrine of election, I believe. God does not simply know what will happen to us, but he is eternally present for everything that has happened and will happen to us.

Thus, God's sovereignty is the basis of our election and salvation. That cause and effect in terms of our faith and salvation may be interchangeable realities from an eternal perspective. Which came first: the chicken or the egg? Perhaps this is always in flux. Just food for thought. In fact, one could argue that God could reveal the future to John the Revelator because He already exists there. Kind of mind-blowing, isn't it? Yet could it be any other way since he is always the Great I AM?

I do not write these things to be critical of my Christians friends or to diminish their witness. Many of them do much more work for the kingdom than I may ever do. I hope that I can remain in fellowship with them regardless of how they feel about my convictions. What I am saying is controversial, and I only offer this perspective on election and salvation as an opinion. Many will understandably take issue with me on these points. Yet I am writing these things for those troubled souls who struggle to embrace God amidst the caricatures of his being, which damages their image of him. I want folks to know that God genuinely loves the world and all in it.

Is Believing in Jesus about Going to Heaven?

What is the ultimate end? Many Christians, particularly conservative ones, say that faith in Christ is about receiving a ticket to heaven. Am I against the idea of going to heaven? Certainly not. However, when you read Paul's letters, he only mentions heaven a few times. This got me to thinking. Then for Paul, what was the end of the Christian faith? We read in Philippians:

> For to me, to live is Christ and to die is gain. If
> I am to go on living in the body, this will mean
> fruitful labor for me. Yet what shall I choose? I
> do not know! I am torn between the two: I desire
> to depart and be with Christ, which is better by

far; but it is more necessary for you that I remain in the body. Convinced of this, I know that I will remain, and I will continue with all of you for your progress and joy in the faith, so that through my being with you again your boasting in Christ Jesus will abound on account of me. (Philippians 1:21–26 NIV)

I think Paul said it best, in so many ways. We are to be united with Christ, united with him in the present and in the life to come. Have you stopped to consider that this might be a different motivation than wanting to play a harp or sing in a heavenly chorus? We read in Philippians, "My goal is to know him and the power of his resurrection and the fellowship of his sufferings, being conformed to his death, assuming that I will somehow reach the resurrection from among the dead" (Philippians 3:10–11 CSB).

For Paul, he did not want to be with Christ so that he could go to heaven; he wanted to go to heaven so that he could be with Christ. There is a fundamental difference in these motivations, isn't there? One focuses on the promise of eternal bliss and the other on an eternal connection. Does that mean there's something wrong with longing for eternal bliss? No, not really, but it misses the larger and more profound point, as I see it.

Salvation is not merely receiving a Get Out of Hell Free card; it's a desire to serve Christ in this life and fellowship with him in the life to come. I am sometimes troubled by evangelical preaching's emphasis on getting out of punishment. Our union with Christ encompasses more fully the meaning of the Gospel, as I see it.

We would then see heaven as an extension of our journey, rather than simply the longed-for destination. Salvation means that the journey that began with our encounter with Jesus will have no end.

As an aside, we do not simply go to heaven; we are "raised with Christ." Many Christians have this notion, not unlike the ancient gnostic heresy, that our soul is trapped in a body of matter.

Upon death, we will be released from this "prison."[14] That is not the image of our resurrection. Paul's ideas about the afterlife are rooted in the Jewish Pharisaic doctrine of resurrection. I not only have a soul, but I am a soul.

My body and spirit comprise a unified being. Paul likened our body to a seed that will eventually die, so that a new organism can live. A seed has within it the germ of life. However, as Paul pointed out, a seed must die so that a stalk of wheat can grow from it. Our body is also a seed. The new organism that grows out of its death is the resurrection body. We are comprised of body, soul, and spirit.

Our soul and spirit draw life and breath from our body. If our body dies, so will our soul and spirit, unless a new body is created from which breath can be drawn. This new body erupts out of the seed of the old one. This is Paul's doctrine of resurrection, and the new body is a spiritual one fashioned after the resurrection body of the Lord.[15] We read again in Philippians, "Our citizenship is in heaven, and we eagerly wait for a Savior from there, the Lord Jesus Christ. He will transform the body of our humble condition into the likeness of his glorious body, by the power that enables him to subject everything to himself" (Philippians 3:20–23 CSB).

We are thus raised to either eternal bliss or everlasting punishment. Our sharing in the Lord's resurrection is the culmination of our spiritual union with him; hopefully, each of us will someday cross that amazing threshold.

What Really Makes Jesus Our Savior?

What was the most difficult challenge for Jesus? Was it to prove that he was authentically God or prove that he was truly man? I am very sure that it was to prove that he was man. Proving that he was God was the easy part. Do a few miracles, wow a few people, and it was in the bag. Yet proving that he was truly man involved entering the vulnerability of the human experience in a way that was convincing; it was the excruciatingly difficult part. It would be like Superman doing everything in his power to demonstrate that he was really Clark Kent.[16]

What was the temptation of Jesus by the devil in the wilderness but an effort to get him to abandon his humanity and use his power to impress the religious, hypnotize the masses, and subdue the powerful? Why? Simply because Satan understood that the mission of Jesus was to identify with humanity and not subdue it.

There have been many messiahs who followed Satan's path: Alexander the Great, Caesar Augustus, and Hitler, among others. Their kingdoms were built on power and conquest, rather than servanthood. It is because of the divinity of Jesus that he is our Lord, but it was because of the humanity of Jesus that he could be our savior.

There is much discussion of the kenotic hymn in Philippians 2:6–8 (CSB), where Paul wrote that Christ, "who existing in the form of God, did not consider equality with God as something to be exploited. Instead he emptied himself by assuming the form of a servant, taking on the likeness of humanity. And when he had come as a man, he humbled himself by becoming obedient to the point of death—even the death of the cross."

This passage has been interpreted many ways. One interpretation is that Jesus emptied himself of his divinity, but that never made sense to me. It is not consistent with the declarations of his divinity found all through the New Testament and the many miracles he performed, which were signs of that divinity.[17]

I like the way the Christian Standard Bible puts it: Christ did not see equality as something to be "exploited," something to be used for his own advantage. I think what Paul is really saying in the kenotic hymn is that Jesus emptied himself of the privileges of divinity, in order to become more fully human, even to the point of experiencing death on a Roman cross. He did not hold onto those privileges as his defining identity but defined his identity by his willingness to enter the reality of the human experience. This was the single most important decision our Lord made, and it affected all the other decisions he made in his life and ministry.

The Importance of the Doctrine of the Divine Logos

When I was fifteen, an older Christian friend introduced me to the prologue of the Gospel of John. In that prologue, I read about the majesty of Jesus, who was the incarnate Word, or Logos, from John 1:1–5 (NIV):

> In the beginning was the Word, and the Word was with God, and the Word was God. He was with God in the beginning. Through him all things were made; without him nothing was made that has been made. In him was life, and that life was the light of all mankind. The light shines in the darkness, and the darkness has not overcome it.

Was the person named Jesus eternal? Actually, no. The eternal Logos was. This is what is really meant by the term "preexistence of Christ." Many Christians do not understand that the incarnation of the Word becoming a man, in the person of Jesus, was a transformative event in the existence of the Triune God. This event is central to the Gospel, as humanity became incorporated into God's very being.

A person named Jesus did not come down from heaven. The eternal Logos became manifest in a historical person named Jesus. The eternal Logos joined with the humanity of Mary to create a unique human being named Jesus. This happened through the assistance of the third person of the Trinity, or the Holy Spirit, as the Gospels have recorded.

Did Jesus return to the same status that the eternal Logos held in the Trinity? No, he did not. He rose to a higher place. Through the incarnation, God the Son became the Son of God, and at the resurrection, the divine Logos, manifested in the divine side of the person of Jesus, and his human side were raised together as one eternal person. Jesus would forever more be both eternal God and eternal man.

He did not return to heaven as the Logos alone but now the Lord Jesus Christ, creating the perfect bridge between our humanity and God's divinity through his own humanity. The Lord Jesus is the one who pleads our case before God as both priest and sacrifice. By becoming flesh, the eternal Logos incorporated humanity into the Triune God, and through Jesus, God the Father can then reach out to us and identify with our humanity, through the humanity of our crucified and risen Lord.[18]

Logos is a philosophical concept; the word comes from the Greek word for "logic" or "organizing principle." This concept became fully developed in the thought of the Jewish philosopher Philo of Alexandria, Egypt, who lived in the first century AD. Philo's ideas are thought to have been influential in the Christology of the early church. Using the reasoning of Plato and Aristotle, Philo viewed the Logos as "the supreme genus of everything that was born."

The Logos is viewed by Philo as God's "shadow," or the instrument of creation. God is the creator of ideas and implementer through His own divine language or Logos, as ideas are both spoken and acted upon in the utterance of God's creative thoughts. The principle of Logos is to establish "specificity" and organization of life and matter. Through the Logos, according to Philo, elements are created (as the ancient world knew them) from "undifferentiated matter" and then become beings and creatures. The world reflects this power but is not a perfect reflection of it; God and the world are not thought to be the same, for only God is uncreated.[19]

The Logos and, now by extension, the Lord Jesus are the agencies of creation. We know from high school physics that matter is atoms in motion, held together by energy. What is the eternal Logos but energy plus intelligence? Jesus is the human incarnation of the eternal Logos, or Word. Colossians 1:17 (NLT) says, "He existed before anything else, and he holds all creation together." *Holds* comes from the Greek word *adhere* (for sticky or glue); he is the glue that holds reality together.

Hebrews 1:3 (ESV) says that Jesus "is the radiance of the glory of God and the exact imprint of his nature. He upholds the universe by the word of His power." We read in the Gospel of John 1:3 (CSB), "All things were created through him, and apart from him not one thing was created that has been created."

When God spoke in Genesis, he did not speak just any word. He spoke *the* Word, and through the agency of that Word, the universe was made and then sustained. Using a *Star Trek* analogy, we are living in God's holodeck, or using an analogy from the movie *The Matrix*, we are living in the matrix that God created and sustains. This word became flesh in the person of Jesus.

Matter itself is not random; atoms and molecules are organized into specific arrangements. Throughout creation, we see the combination of matter, energy, and information. Without energy and information, neither inanimate matter nor organic life could exist. This speaks to the mystery of the eternal Logos. The creative embodiment and vehicle of God's power and organizing intelligence are merged into a series of divine actions (over a period of six days), which are implemented when God speaks a word.

Human ingenuity requires energy, effort, planning, time, and patience. We can build a skyscraper when we combine our intelligence with time, effort, machines, fuel, resources, and workers. However, God could speak a skyscraper into existence, combining all the above powers into a single instantaneous act. That is, in fact, how God created the universe.

An enormous amount of energy is required for matter to even exist. According to one of our physical laws, "neither matter nor energy can be created or destroyed." They are interchangeable states. We see, for example, what happens when energy is liberated from just a few thousand pounds of uranium: Enough energy is released to either power an entire city or level one. Consider for a moment how much energy is present in the matter of the earth, our solar system, our sun, and indeed our universe. More energy is required to hold all of this together than any of us can possibly imagine, much less measure.

Matter itself is not random but organized and linked together by electrical bonds. Matter is composed of specific components we call elements, which can be reduced to their constituent atoms and building blocks. Our periodic table of elements is a chart of these atomic building blocks. Doesn't the organization of matter itself suggest an imbedded intelligence?

When two or more components of matter are put together, a molecule is formed. Molecules are the forms of matter that occur from such combinations of the constituent building blocks. Let us take water as an example. Water is H_2O, a molecule comprised of one atom of oxygen and two atoms of hydrogen. Water can be in a liquid, solid, or gas state, depending on the strength and movement of its electrical bonds based on cold or heat. No other molecule will form into water; thus, the existence of water requires a specific arrangement of atoms. There is nothing random about it.

God's power created, bonded, and organized matter into the patterns we know. All God has to do is speak out the divine Logos or Word, and things happen instantaneously because intelligence, planning, energy, and effort are merged into a single creative act, incorporating all of the above at once. It's implemented by the speaking or transmission of a word.

Computers are intelligent because they are programmed with languages such as FORTRAN, COBOL, PASCAL, or Java. The world and the universe are also programmed with a language, called the eternal LOGOS, or eternal logic.

This eternal vehicle of God's programming became incarnate in a human being called Jesus of Nazareth. He shared God's thoughts and was literally a reflection of His will and purpose and yet distinct as the one who is coeternal, even as God's thoughts, words, and power are a coeternal part of his nature.

For instance, is the classic book *The Iliad* a work separate from Homer or an embodiment of the Greek author's words, thoughts, sentiments, and efforts? The book as an entity is distinct from Homer, but it embodies everything that he was. This is also true of God and the coeternal word. Yet the eternal Logos and coeternal

Son are living embodiments of the Father's purpose; they are not a thing but a person who shares in his very life and being. The Word or Logos proceeded from the Father but was distinct from the Father as the agent of creation.

Yet how many people in church who love Jesus as the Creator have never had the deeper mystery behind the incarnation explained to them? Am I splitting hairs here? Possibly. Is it a mistaken idea that diminishes the Christian witness of anyone? I don't think so, but understanding this mystery helps all of us appreciate even more the word from Colossians 2:9–10 (NIV), "For in Christ the fullness of the Deity lives in bodily form."

As a Christian pilgrim, I am troubled that we don't bother to educate the average Christian person, in terms of how glorious our creator and savior truly are. Many look to see where God is, when I would wonder where God is not. This is the same creator who promised us that by his word, a new earth and heaven will emerge. All he needs to do is let go of creation, and all things will implode. We see this in the final judgment:

> But the day of the Lord will come as unexpectedly as a thief. Then the heavens will pass away with a terrible noise, and the very elements themselves will disappear in fire, and the earth and everything on it will be found to deserve judgment. (1 Peter 3:10 NLT)

Chapter 2
SIN, SATAN, AND DIVINE CONNECTIONS

Sin Is More Than Just about Making the Wrong Choices

Most biblically based churches repeat a fundamental misunderstanding about the meaning of the Fall and original sin. This error is forgivable and understandable, but it's an error, nonetheless. What was the real root of Adam's character flaw, a flaw so deep that God cast him and Eve out of the garden?

If you recall from the Genesis story, God gives Adam and Eve a single command: Do not eat from the Tree of the Knowledge of Good and Evil, or they will die. The serpent (many Christians interpret this as Satan, but there is only a passing reference to this) tells Eve to eat of the tree, and she will be like God. I prefer the KJV translation of Genesis 3:5 here: "And ye shall be as gods, knowing good and evil."

This KJV rendering foreshadows the development of pagan mythology, as humans project their image upon fabricated deities who share their flaws, including vanity. Eve offers the fruit to Adam, who is enticed by the sales job Eve does on behalf of the serpent. After they both eat, they become aware of their nakedness and fashion clothes out of fig leaves.

God calls out for them in the cool of the evening, but Adam and Eve are afraid to answer; they hide from God, who finds them and asks Adam why he disobeyed him. The first thing he does is blame Eve: "Well, if it wasn't for that woman you gave me, I never would have thought to eat it." God in turn asks Eve, who explains that the serpent was to blame. In other words, "The devil made me do it." This prompted God to throw them out of the garden.

Why, just because the first couple simply made a bad choice? No, not really. It is because neither took moral responsibility for their actions. At the heart of sin is not simply the propensity to make bad choices but the evasion of moral responsibility accompanying those choices.

For example, King David was considered a man after God's own heart. Was it because he was more virtuous than others? No, quite the opposite. It was because he responded to his horrendous actions with a deep remorse and repentance. King David took moral responsibility for his actions. David wrote these words: "Create in me a clean heart, O God. Renew a loyal spirit within me" (Psalm 51:10 NLT). Can you hear any remorse in the words of Adam or Eve? Any regret? Any responsibility for their actions? Any desire to make things right?

That numbness and evasion of moral responsibility was at the heart of their sin. In prison, it's amusing how often you hear claims of innocence. Sometimes, those protestations reflect the truth, but often, they reflect an unwillingness to accept blame for wrongdoing.

In fact, the blame shifting that Adam and Eve engaged in is practically a hallmark of criminality. It is always someone else's fault. I was enticed and framed. I had a bad childhood, and so forth, even though those reasons may be valid. Just as a wise man once said when watching the hanging of a thief, "There but for the grace of God, go I."

Yet those reasons are proffered as a standard explanation. They are not. In 1945, a US marshal from Missouri gave President Harry Truman a desk plaque with these words: "The buck stops here." This plaque signified President Truman's tenacity in taking responsibility for tough issues.[20] A similar plaque could have been nailed to the top of the cross, along with "King of the Jews." The buck was stopping with Jesus. No more evasions. No more rationalizations. Jesus was going to take responsibility, and his shoulders were big enough to take responsibility for the whole world.

What to Do with Satan

Some view the devil as a metaphor or personification of evil, and others see him as a literal being. I have waffled on this issue but now come down firmly on believing the latter. Why? Perhaps because I have had too many battles with this person throughout my life to deny his reality. 1 Peter 5:8 (NIV) states that the devil comes like "a roaring lion," ready to eat us alive. Paul advised the church in Ephesians 6:11 (NLT) to put on "God's armor" to battle the devil's numerous strategies.

We need to acknowledge some important facts about Satan. He is wiser than us, and he has existed for millennia. He is more powerful than us and is attuned to our every weakness. He knows where we're vulnerable. Why would God allow such a malignant being to continue existing? There is an aspect of mystery to this, I think.

However, the answer may be that God loves everything he created, including fallen angels. Second, it has always been God's intention to honor the free will of his beings. He sought to create a real world where the possibilities of choosing between good and evil would be continually present, even for divine servants.

Satan has drawn me into many battles and has won quite a few, frankly. Why is that? First, because he is more powerful than we are. Second, as Paul expressed in 2 Corinthians 11:14 (NIV), Satan "masquerades" as an "angel of light" to us. He is not the ugly red-skinned, horned caricature of *Dante's Inferno* or Halloween.

Satan is the accuser; he enters our consciousness and attempts to bring despair to our thinking by reminding us of our faults. He seeks to indict us on that basis, as if the forgiveness of God was not a reality. We read in Revelation, "Then I heard a loud voice in heaven say: 'Now have come the salvation and the power and the kingdom of our God, and the authority of his Messiah. For the accuser of our brothers and sisters, who accuses them before our God day and night, has been hurled down'" (Revelation 12:10 NIV).

Satan is our accuser, and in fact, he is very clever at playing on our pride, conceit, and self-righteousness. He is very cruel in bringing to our mind our failures, sin, and vulnerabilities. He does this to bring us into despair or cause us to protect our pride. Once he has done this, we are well defeated.

Yet I have found the way to defeat him. Imagine for a moment that I am having a conversation with Satan:

He says to me, "Robert, I know about your secret sins. I know what you are insecure about."

I could deny it, of course, but what if I said, "You know what? You are right."

Satan could then look triumphant and say, "Well, then, you know you are defeated, right?"

I could then say, "No, not really."

He would retort, "What do you mean?"

I would conclude the conversation by saying, "You see, Satan, I am going to joyfully proclaim my weakness to you, for as Paul says in 2 Corinthians 12:9 (NIV), 'My grace is sufficient for you, for my power is made perfect in weakness.'"

Satan, I gladly declare my weakness so that Christ's power can flow through it. Try what you will, Satan, you are not fighting me anymore, and who I have unleashed you cannot defeat. So get lost.

As a final thought, Satan can speak through other people as well. He can be that voice of doubt that tells us our efforts are pointless and life is meaningless. Truthfully, in our world, we hear many voices. However, the voice of truth, as my wife likes to describe it, comes to us in a "still small voice" (1 Kings 19:12 KJV), as it did to Elijah in the cave.

This is one reason I advocate for silent retreats, where you can get away from the boisterous noise of our culture, and the noise inside of your head. You are then more likely to hear the encouraging voice of God instead of the discouraging voice of the evil one.

What Is the Difference between Jesus and Myth?

C. S. Lewis wrote that in Jesus, "all the myths of the world are made true."[21] However, I would say that in Jesus, the myths of the world are turned on their heads. What are mythological gods but beings full of human qualities, granted great powers, and projected upon an imagined deity? What is Zeus but the embodiment of Greek ideals? Jupiter of Roman ones? Osiris of Egyptian ones, and so forth. Yet what is Jesus then? Is he not what happened when an actual deity projected his image upon an actual human?

A person who was a contradiction of cultural ideals and vanity instead of an embodiment of them, someone who authentically embodied otherworldly values. Jesus was the incarnate refutation of the world's myths. Here a human image is created that we are called to worship as Lord; he comes to love and serve, and demands nothing of us that he himself was not also willing to do.

Jesus is not a god demanding that we build him a temple with a statue of his likeness or sacrifice our livestock, worldly goods, or children to him. Jesus hugs animals and loves children. Jesus, in fact, is disheartened by the corruption of the worldly temple in Jerusalem. He did not come to wipe out or destroy our enemies, either, and he wholeheartedly resisted such a proposition. Jesus sacrifices himself to the violence of others.

Summarizing this point, Jesus does not fit human mythology. He contradicts it. Satan offers Jesus worldly glory if he would only bow to his agenda, which Jesus refuses to do. Satan understood what the people wanted from their mythological gods. Satan himself, as I see it, is the power behind these imaginary deities and deceives us as to how the real God became incarnate in Jesus, as it is written in 2 Corinthians:

> Satan, who is the god of this world, has blinded the minds of those who don't believe. They are unable to see the glorious light of the Good News. They don't understand this message about the glory of Christ, who is the exact likeness of God. (2 Corinthians 4:4 NLT)

The imaginary gods wanted favors, power, and spectacle. Jesus gave humanity something greater than any imagined god. He gave of himself and his own person. Demigods like Hercules reveled in their powers, but Jesus celebrated his humanity and weakness. In Jesus, we see a person and a divine being who distinguished himself from the rest of humanity, not by his power per se, but by his capacity to love.

Jesus distinguishes himself not by his capacity to stand above us but by his intention to stand with us. Jesus is what happens when the most powerful being in the universe comes to share with us that power is not what the divine being values the most. Love and humility are.

When Jesus uses his powers, it is not to solicit favors or revel in his great powers, as the gods of mythology were apt to do, but to demonstrate his love and compassion. He does not come to demand that the world serve him; instead, he came to serve the world and the two other members of the Triune God, his Father and the Holy Spirit, whom he loved and was faithful to. The gods of mythology were often jealous of each other, vying for humanity to choose between them, but the members of the Triune God do nothing but share with each other, support each other, and love each other. The Father, Son, and Holy Spirit exist to bring glory and honor to each other. Jesus exhorted his followers to love the Father and Spirit as they loved him.

Finally, Jesus threatens no one with retribution or violence; ultimately, he hands himself over to the violence of human beings, to show the lengths to which love will go, to demonstrate that it is stronger than hate or human sin. Oddly enough, that is what you do not see in the character of the mythological gods. They are powerful, muscular, and threatening, not unlike our modern mythology of superheroes.

We see in actual mythology that the gods are the created beings, and we are the creators. The incarnation shows us that we are the created beings, and the incarnate Logos is the creator, and he comes not to awe us but to love us.

The Incarnation Was about Identifying with the Tragedy of Our Human Condition

Who has believed what he has heard from us? And to whom has the arm of the Lord been revealed? For he grew up before him like a young plant, and like a root out of dry ground; he had no form or majesty that we should look at him, and no beauty that we should desire him.

He was despised and rejected by men, a man of sorrows and acquainted with grief, and as one from whom men hide their faces, he was despised, and we esteemed him not.

Surely, he has borne our griefs and carried our sorrows; yet we esteemed him stricken, smitten by God, and afflicted.

But he was pierced for our transgressions; he was crushed for our iniquities; upon him was the chastisement that brought us peace, and with his wounds we are healed. All we like sheep have gone astray; we have turned—every one—to his own way; and the Lord has laid on him the iniquity of us all. (Isaiah 53:1–6 ESV)

Isaiah was the book that Jesus quoted the most in terms of his mission and his own self-understanding. Isaiah has been called the Gospel of the Old Testament. I can understand that for sure, since it contains so many jewels that relate well to the themes of mercy, forgiveness, and the reign of God's kingdom. I love Isaiah as well for its poetry, and most of all for its imagery. It is a book that truly captivates the reader. Isaiah 53 is quite captivating.

Jewish exegetes have traditionally attributed this passage as a symbolic representation of the suffering servant Jewish people. I remember at a ministerial association meeting, a conservative rabbi shared with me that "as Jews, we know nothing of a messiah who suffers."

Yes, to attribute this passage to the messiah was truly revolutionary. The messiah was going to suffer as we do. Therefore, few Jewish religious leaders were prepared to embrace the claims of a prophet who would assert this image from Isaiah, as the hallmark of his messianic authority.

Many sermons have been preached and commentaries written about Isaiah 53. However, what I find conspicuously absent and troubling is the omission of how this passage relates to you and me. This passage, or so we believe, is a picture of Jesus, a picture from the inside out, a portrait of his character, appearance, and emotions. I am going to digress into a sermon here but one that I hope you find uplifting.

First, Jesus grew up. You know that phase of life filled with hope, excitement, angst, and frustration. Do you think Jesus was oblivious to this period of human existence? No. As we read in Isaiah 53:1 (ESV), "For he grew up before him like a young plant, and like a root out of dry ground." Like Adam, Jesus was made from the dust of the ground. He struggled to live and to relate to his peers and to obey his parents. Jesus says to those of us who still suffer the pains of childhood that he too knows those pains.

Jesus was not a naturally attractive person, either, if we take this passage as an authentic picture. Sometimes, we can think little of ourselves, especially in a culture that sets up certain people to be idols of physical perfection and glamour. We can look in the mirror and tell ourselves, "I am ugly." Jesus says to those of us who may see ourselves as ugly that he had no appearance that would draw anyone to him, and no great handsomeness or glamor, either.

There are few things worse in this life than rejection, especially to be rejected by those whose approval and adoration we long for the most. This can be approval from a mom or dad, from an organization, or from a group of friends, where we long to find inclusion. We can become medicated with drugs to numb the pain of our depression and loneliness.

We may protest how God does not understand living with that kind of pain, but Jesus responds to us by saying that he was also hated and rejected by many. A person who had experienced terrible grief and who felt ostracized by those who misunderstood him, even by the very brethren he longed to have a relationship with the most.

It was not just our sins that Jesus carried in his life and death but also our grief. Jesus carrying the grief of the world; it was a big part of the atonement he made on our behalf. The wounds of Jesus heal our sin, but more importantly, he came to heal us of grief, the kind of grief that comes from being judged by a cruel world, and the self-judgment that's been formed in us by that cruelty. Jesus wants to form in us a different way of looking at the world, which begins by looking at ourselves differently.

We could then see that we don't have to look at ourselves as unattractive, depressed, or unsuccessful, as some have deemed it; it's not the only way we can live, and the creator has a completely different criteria for evaluating our lives than society does. This criteria, as I see it, was put into the incarnation itself so we could see what God values in the world and, more importantly, how he values each of us, as flawed as we may believe ourselves to be.

As a Christian pilgrim, I am sometimes troubled by how many Christians I encounter who still judge themselves, and others, by the shallow criteria of our society. Our Lord Jesus showed us that there is no greater beauty than that which radiates from within. The ministry of Jesus was, in fact, to make that very point.

Chapter 3

CHURCH UNITY AND CHURCH SCHISM: A LITTLE BIT OF HISTORY AND PERSPECTIVE

How Liberals and Fundamentalists Are Both Wrong in Their View of the Bible

I grew up in a mainline church, but back in 1979, I was introduced to evangelical theology by the magazine *Christianity Today*. I was sent a subscription by a messianic Jew who visited my home church that year. I also had a deeply devout grandmother who shared her faith in Jesus with us and cited passages to us from her Schofield Reference Bible.

Around the same time, I became involved with a couple of older friends who introduced me to the Jesus movement. It was a charismatic movement that emphasized home Bible worship, Bible study, being filled with the Holy Spirit, and speaking in tongues. They were pejoratively called "Jesus freaks."[22]

They used guitars and nontraditional worship, which I will talk about later. They shared with me the prologue to the Gospel of John and told me about the gifts of the Holy Spirit. The son of one of our church members spoke convincingly of physical healings and not paying attention to human interpretations of the Bible. I was not popular in school, nor was I the best student, but I felt a sense of belonging at these home-based charismatic worship services, unlike anything I had previously experienced.

What impressed me was the sense of God's immediacy and power that these Jesus freaks had, along with idea that God could make his Word known to us through the pages of the Bible. It was at this time that my excitement about the Bible and what God could communicate through it began to grip me.

I became very fascinated by the various gifts listed in the New Testament, something never spoken of in the churches I had attended. I wondered why I had not been made aware of all this in my religious instruction. Later I would learn how many church communions formed and split over just such issues.

Apparently, certain things from the Bible were clearer to some than others. The dispensational school, which produced the beloved Schofield Bible, argued that spiritual gifts, like tongues, ceased with the apostolic age. First Corinthians 13 is cited in support of such a position.

> Love never fails. But where there are prophecies, they will cease, where there are tongues, they will be stilled; where there is knowledge, it will pass away. (1 Corinthians 13:8 NIV)

Yet, upon examining the context of such a passage, it became clear that Paul was trying to put gifts in their proper perspective and not argue that they were part of a passing dispensation or past system of order, as we read, "I would like every one of you to speak in tongues, but I would rather have you prophesy. The one who prophesies is greater than the one who speaks in tongues, unless someone interprets, so that the church may be edified" (1 Corinthians 14:5 NIV).

I began to learn that there was quite a bit of divergence, even among conservative Christians, about numerous spiritual and doctrinal issues. A history professor once said, "Inerrancy does not settle everything." Putting it differently, just because something is in the Bible, and we agree on our beliefs about the nature of the Bible, does not mean we are going to look at things the same way.

Interpretation matters and is influenced by the traditions we embrace, such as the ordination of women, the role of the pastor in congregational life, and what kind of church government best reflects the spirit of the New Testament. Does the priesthood of the believer grant the laity a role in ministry? Should the Creation account in Genesis be taken as literal history or symbolic representation? Are spiritual gifts still valid and relevant today? These are some of the differences we find among Christians who believe in scriptural inspiration. These issues were also debated in the seminary I attended.

I was a seminary student back in the late 1980s. I was a mainline Christian student in an alternative theological school during a tumultuous time in the history of the sponsoring denomination. There was a schism between liberals in the denomination who embraced historical critical studies, or what is called higher criticism, of the Bible and conservatives who believed in verbal inspiration.

The former group believed that the Bible could be examined as a patchwork of various sources woven together by editors, often reflecting conflicting perspectives and contrasting theological reflections. The conservatives believed that the perfections of God were reflected in the biblical texts themselves.

Shortly after beginning seminary, I joined an evangelical group that met on the campus and soon realized that I had become involved with the campus pariahs, who drew me into the center of a political conflict that soon took over the seminary. We met periodically with the school president in the cafeteria. One afternoon, after such a meeting, a member of this evangelical group saw me and said, "You might want to stay away from us; the president just hung us out to dry."

I later learned that the president's ire was directed at the evangelical group for meeting with a pastor from Virginia, who offered to help reconcile the conflict. I was in the middle of a controversy concerning the inspiration and interpretation of the Bible.

The centrist group in charge of the school embraced the position known as neoorthodoxy, even though they were mainly evangelical in their theology. I knew a little a bit about neoorthodoxy. I had written a paper about Karl Barth my senior year at the college I attended in Virginia. My favorite professor, a scholar in history, allowed me to write my senior reflection paper on Barth. I greatly enjoyed talking with this instructor, who was one of the leading authorities on medieval councils in the world. He was also an exceptional Christian.

I poured through several books, including Barth's monumental multivolume work entitled *The Church Dogmatics*. He was influenced by a movement called existentialism, a system of philosophy that emphasizes the truths that are communicated through existence, experiences, and encounters. This school of thought included both theistic and atheistic philosophers; Barth was influenced by Soren Kierkegaard, a nineteenth-century Christian existentialist from Denmark.

Kierkegaard emphasized the seemingly absurd and cruel demands that God made on his followers, for example, when he demanded that Abraham sacrifice his son Isaac, and then the Lord disclosed that it was Abraham's faith that was being tested and that no sacrifice would actually be required.

Barth was steeped in the liberal theology of the Tubingen school in Germany, which studied the Bible like any other ancient document, parceling it out according to its possible sources and viewing supernatural claims and events with skepticism. The value of the Bible lay in its ability to model an evolving human consciousness that brings us closer to God's purpose for us, as exemplified especially by Jesus.

This was the view of premier liberal theologian Friedrich

Schleiermacher, as expressed in his seminal work *Christianity and Its Cultured Despisers*. Germany saw itself as part of the growing Christian consciousness being advanced through its culture. Then World War I happened, and Barth saw his professors at Tubingen enthusiastically supporting the kaiser's war ambitions. This precipitated a spiritual crisis in Barth's life, whereby he began to question the very foundation of his Christian convictions. Like Luther before him, he went to Romans to find an answer and found a key verse:

> The wrath of God is being revealed from heaven against all the godlessness and wickedness of people, who suppress the truth by their wickedness. (Romans 1:18 NIV)

Barth finished his pivotal commentary on the book of Romans in 1919, and out of his new insight about the disconnection between revelation and human culture, he developed neoorthodoxy, a new existential paradigm of Christian theology and biblical interpretation. Historical critical study of the Bible was still valid; however, although the Word of God was present in the Bible, those words became the Word of God to us in an encounter with the Word behind the words.

Thus, the Bible could be flawed in its presentation but could serve as an instrument of a divine encounter. Barth's theology emphasized the discontinuity between revelation and human experience. Human experience was more likely an expression of the sins and vices of humanity, rather than a reflection of divine purpose, as classical Christian liberalism appeared to be arguing. Twentieth-century mainline Christianity, including the denominations that I grew up in, reordered its theology along neoorthodoxy lines.[23]

Starting in the late nineteenth century, another movement emerged against liberal theology known as fundamentalism. Taking its cues from scholastic theology, it argued that God's divine breath was so thoroughly present in the writers of scripture that the Lord's perfections can be seen in the Bible, right down to the words selected to express a divine truth. This position had both uneducated and highly educated champions. We read in 2 Timothy:

> All Scripture is breathed out by God and profitable for teaching, for reproof, for correction, and for training in righteousness. (2 Timothy 3:16 ESV)

We further read in 1 Corinthians:

> We have not received the spirit of the world, but the Spirit who is from God, that we may understand what God has freely given us. And this is what we speak, not words taught us by human wisdom, but words taught by the Spirit, expressing spiritual truths in spiritual words. (1 Corinthians 2:12–13 BSB)

The best-known advocates were the theologians from Princeton Theological Seminary, such as Archibald Hodge, Charles Hodge, and Benjamin Warfield. These men were amazing theologians. My dad bought me Hodge's three-volume theology back in 1985. In Benjamin Warfield's *Studies in Augustine and Tertullian*, I learned about church father Tertullian's understanding of the Trinity and developed my own understanding of Logos Christology.

These Princeton theologians argued that the truth of the Bible could be plainly understood through reason and context. As Hodge himself once wrote, "Any error in the Bible was about as significant as the fragments surrounding a carved statue."[24]

While I was in seminary, much of the debate about inerrancy was centered on a conference put on by my seminary's sponsoring denomination, in response to the *Chicago Statement on Biblical Inerrancy* in 1987, which was largely a modern restatement of the classical Hodge-Warfield position on biblical inspiration. The Creation account was to be taken literally (although Warfield was open to evolution), along with the Flood account and everything in the first eleven chapters of Genesis. Its backers included luminaries like conservative Anglican James I. Packer, R. C. Sproul, Francis Schaeffer, Dr. Carl F. H. Henry, and the Rev. E. V. Hill. I knew Packer, Schaeffer, and Henry from *Christianity Today*.[25] Centrists and conservatives in the denomination attended this conference to find some middle ground on this issue.

Later, the centrist president of my seminary attended a conference out West, where a joint statement was issued in an effort to find an area of reconciliation. The statement expressed the sentiment that the Bible could not mislead anyone.

I was particularly a fan of the late Dr. Carl F. H. Henry, the theologian who undergirded the religious movement of Billy Graham and helped him found *Christianity Today*. I had the opportunity to meet him twice, first at a Baptist church where he preached and then at a Methodist conference where he emphasized that inerrancy was the path to biblical fidelity. He urged me to read the earlier issues of *Christianity Today*, when it was genuinely conservative.[26]

Sadly, my seminary was torn apart by this very inerrancy issue, and it became increasingly difficult not to take a side in the controversy. I helped to organize a service in the main chapel of the school, but that did little to inspire reconciliation. Our president resigned shortly thereafter because he could not find a middle ground with most of the trustees of the institution.

The seminary brought in a new president who was endorsed by Graham. I wrote both the new president and Billy Graham, thanking them for their contributions and hoping that their ministry would bring peace to the campus. I received a nice letter from the president and the personal secretary of Dr. Graham, thanking me for my letter.

The new president was formally installed a couple of months prior to my graduation. A seminary friend of mine and I went to visit the new leader shortly after he came to the campus. He said to us, "Let me share with you a little secret. All of the early … theologians were inerrantists, brother."

Dr. Graham was the keynote speaker at the new president's inauguration. I walked through a crowd of protestors to enter the chapel and felt dreadful about crossing their protests, but it occurred to me that this might be my only opportunity to see Dr. Graham in person (as it turned out, it was). I was not going to deny myself that experience. I took photos of Dr. Graham as he passed my pew in the procession with a school trustee. Graham was a man of large stature and spoke of how the school could be "a light to the world."

Many dignitaries came to the campus, including the president of the denomination and conservative professors from outside the school. The bitterness did not subside but only increased because many perceived Dr. Graham as a pawn in the trustees' effort to make the school into an inerrantist institution.[27] Bumper stickers were printed in memory of the ousted centrist administration, comparing the expulsion with a famous battle in history.

I confess, it became difficult for me to maintain my relationships on campus across that bitter divide. This ugliness culminated in a student asking me how I liked taking the denomination's money. This was a reference to a grant that had paid for most of my seminary tuition. I cried and sobbed that entire fateful day.

Yet, I confess, some of the more liberal professors could be quite ugly in depicting inerrantists as people who presented the Bible as "a holy Koran," with no humanity or complexity. As I look back on that drama, I realize that there were wrong-headed and sympathetic people on both sides, and it has only taken me several years to put my finger on why.

I found pursuing the ministry in the school's sponsoring denomination difficult because of the theological controversy, although I would serve three churches as a licensed minister in the Methodist Church and become ordained in the Gospel ministry. I would also serve, briefly, as a pastor of a mission church in one of the mid-Atlantic states. The biggest mark against me at the time was that I was single. That topic is for my next book.

In 1995, I came back to the mainline church I grew up in, through a special call process. I flew up to North Carolina from Florida to meet with a denominational executive and a ministry committee at a local congregation, to approve my call. I was told by a former Southern Baptist that "the waters were good in my mainline church" and that my former, late pastor "was a very persuasive fellow." I was excited to finally be approved for general ministry in my former denomination and to have an ecclesiastical home.

I served as a pastor from 1996 to 2004. Those were rewarding and exciting years. However, during that same time, something was stirring at the national level of my beloved mainline church. Whereas some denominations had shifted to the right, during this same period, the denomination I grew up in was drifting in the opposite direction. Many embraced what I perceive as a socially and theologically radical direction.

The denomination even had an essay contest in the early 2000s around the theme of a "continually speaking God." I wrote and submitted an essay that if God were speaking, he would want a church that was intentionally countercultural to the trends of society. I never heard back from the national headquarters of my denomination about my essay. However, a friend of mine, who was ordained in the Reformed Church of America, used my essay as a basis for a lay course he once taught. Oh, well, genius is never appreciated by some (I'm being sarcastic).

The leadership of my beloved mainline church home was turning what had been a relatively inclusive denomination into one that conservative and even moderate folks were bound to find uncomfortable. Biblical studies became historical critical methodology on steroids.

The way I saw the trend, there did not appear to be an internal critique going on at the denominational level about the agendas that were being pursued in the name of scholarship or questionable liberal trends in theological studies. Those who raised such issues were often dismissed as out of touch with modern trends, like a conservative group in my beloved denomination, comprised of members and clergy who advocated for an evangelical witness within the denomination.

The mainline church was going down a road started in 1985 by a group of scholars organized under Robert Funk, who launched the Jesus seminar. This endeavor was an attempt to discover what could be known about Jesus based on source material research; along with many unknown scholars, it had some prominent theologians like John Dominic Crossan and Marcus Borg. However, the Jesus seminar was primarily comprised of unknown scholars from various liberal institutions, like Vanderbilt and Claremont theological seminaries.

Based on a study of sources, the seminar even asserted that the apocryphal gospel of Thomas might have more original source material in it than the Gospel of John. Also, the seminar claimed that Jesus was not concerned about an apocalypse or the end of the world or time.

Just to illustrate how ridiculous the seminar got, they would color code certain passages of the Gospels and claim according to one color Jesus definitely said and did this, according to another color, Jesus probably said and did this, and according to yet another color, Jesus most likely did not say or do this. How comforting it is that we have the Jesus seminar to help us know for certain what Jesus said and did (I'm being sarcastic again).

While Marcus Borg was a man of some piety, Robert Funk went so far as to assert that the "dead body of Jesus was thrown into an empty grave." I do wonder who that was supposed to bring comfort to.[28] The criticism of the seminar from mainstream scholars was torrential, starting with Catholic scholar Raymond Brown, who essentially said it was bunk.[29] N. T. Wright, Luke Timothy Johnson, and others saw it as a new fundamentalism, taking seriously only those texts that could be definitively traced back as authentic. It was, in fact, not a scholarly panel at all but a theological statement. I would dub it the Chicago Statement of liberal Christianity.

Years ago, I attended a pastor conference down in Key West, Florida. The keynote speaker was William R. Herzog of Colgate Rochester Divinity School in New York. Herzog was an American Baptist professor of New Testament studies. I asked him during one of our breaks what he thought of the Jesus seminar. He told me, and I paraphrase from memory, "The Jesus seminar attempted to deconstruct the faith of the church. I am a theologian of the church, and the faith of the church is what I am about. That is what I think of the Jesus seminar." In other words, Dr. Herzog could not stomach an agenda in scholarship that was primarily theological and anti- church tradition, to boot.

A couple years later, I watched a video highlighting how Christianity could become relevant and humane again, by liberating itself from the need to adhere to ancient dogmas, thanks to the findings of the Jesus seminar. Sounded a lot like the old liberalism of the early twentieth century, dressed in new clothes.[30]

We can see the move toward liberalism in scrapping the designations of BC and AD in favor of BCE and CE. BC meant "Before Christ." That is easy enough. However, there is some confusion with AD, as some people may believe it means "After Death" of Jesus. This is an understandable misnomer, but the real meaning of the initials comes from the Latin words *Anno Domini*, which means in English "in the year of our Lord." BCE means "Before Common Era" and CE means "Common Era."

This calendar designation was often used by Jewish people to distance themselves from the Christian connotation of our calendar, and I can understand their reasons. However, when Christians do it, it just sounds like persnickety liberalism. Yes, this is a pet peeve of mine, but what is wrong with acknowledging that our calendar proclaims the Gospel?[31]

At this point, you may be thinking, *This guy sure has spent a lot more time on this section than the others.* I appreciate your patience with me. Why did I do it? I was endeavoring to show you what I call the bookends of biblical studies. You have the Jesus freaks on one bookend and the Jesus seminar on the other. Barth is somewhere in the middle of the bookshelf. There is a lot to explore here, more than I care to cover. I encourage you to read up about these topics. It will not be light reading, but it's very educational.

An author named William Willimon once said that fundamentalism and liberalism were "two sides of the same modernist coin." One was going to use reason to assert that the Bible was a perfect revelation and the other by reason that the Bible at best is an inconsistent one. Yet what if both are essentially wrong? What makes the Bible powerful in the lives of people? Is it not the power of the scriptures to be self-authenticating? The Bible proves itself, as I see it, to be the Word of God, by its spiritual power and the influence that its narrative story has on those who digest it and act on its truths.

The Bible was written by a community: first, the community of the Jews, and then, the community of the church. While our book belongs to each of us, collectively, it belongs to the church and speaks for the faith of the church. That the same Spirit who inspired the writers to write it also opens our minds and hearts to receive its message. Paul wrote that without the Spirit, our hearts are closed to spiritual truth.[32]

> The natural man does not accept the things that come from the Spirit of God. For they are foolishness to him, and he cannot understand them because they are spiritually discerned. (1 Corinthians 2:14 BSB)

John Calvin made the point that human intellect is darkened by sin and therefore needs the work of the Spirit to receive anything from the scriptures.[33] It is neither a Koran nor a mere book but a chronicle of events across the history of a people, which involved the mighty acts of God.

I remember my late pastor, from the church I grew up in,

ruminating about how it is the humanity of the biblical characters and their stories that made them seem so real and believable. A beloved professor of mine once shared in preaching class that the Bible reflected the brokenness of the human experience. One of my objections to the way biblical studies are framed is that any admission of humanity in our scriptures is viewed as a mark against it being an authentic repository and vehicle of revelation.

Let us consider the bookends for a moment. The Chicago Statement and the Jesus seminar seem to hold one conviction in common: that any admission of humanity in our Bible presents a problem in believing in it as a receptacle of revelatory disclosure, or a book that God speaks through with authority. As a troubled pilgrim, I have wondered why the humanity of our Bible is perceived as a reason to doubt its inspiration.

I do not believe in the Bible because it reflects a cleverly written mythology or simply because of claims made about it. The Bible is its own best advocate. I believe it because it tells of real human beings, encountering extraordinary revelations, in a way that is convincing and believable. The Bible is an incarnational revelation. Just as Jesus was both authentically man and God with the tensions that creates, the Bible is both the Word of God and the word of man, with the tensions that creates. Human beings became the earthen vessels that God poured his revelation into:

> But we have this treasure in earthen vessels, so that the surpassing greatness of the power will be of God and not from ourselves. (2 Corinthians 4:7 NASB)

Many can wonder why there is some discrepancy in the accounts of our Gospels. Well, there usually is some discrepancy in the real stories of eyewitness accounts. That is the actual human story. That is the real human experience. It is only in well-crafted stories, fables, or myths that you get perfect collaboration. We read in 2 Peter:

> For we were not making up clever stories when we
> told you about the powerful coming of our Lord
> Jesus Christ. We saw his majestic splendor with
> our own eyes. (2 Peter 1:16 NLT)

Unlike Barth, I am sure that the Bible is the Word of God, objectively speaking. Unlike Warfield and Hodge, I do not think that the Bible can be received or understood through reason alone. They are both partially correct, in my opinion. It is objectively the word of God, but it does not become the word of God for me until I receive it for myself through the opening of my eyes and heart by the Holy Spirit, until it touches my humanity. There is both the objective Word of God and our subjective encounter with it as readers and pilgrims.

Is there any benefit to historical critical analysis? Well, I have studied it, and I am not averse to looking at sources or assessing how materials were gathered or examining the textual difficulties present, in what is called lower criticism. The idea is acceptable to me that the last part of the Gospel of Mark or the story of the "woman caught in adultery" found in the Gospel of Luke may have been added or inserted after those Gospels had already been written. Those facts do not negate the inspiration of the insertions, either.

However, there are two fundamental flaws this troubled pilgrim has seen in higher criticism. First, there is a prejudice among some scholars when it comes to the miraculous stories in the Old Testament and New Testament. Second, we should be aware that the Holy Spirit, who inspired the scriptures, plays an essential role in our understanding of them. The Bible became alive for me when I became alive.

We see recorded in the Gospel of John that Jesus promised that the Holy Spirit would assist the apostles in understanding and in remembering the Lord's teaching.

> But the Advocate, the Holy Spirit, whom the
> Father will send in my name, and teach you all

things and will remind you of everything I have said to you. (John 14:26 NIV)

You might dispute that the miracles witnessed were miracles in the supernatural sense. We are talking about ancient perceptions, after all, but it is hard to dispute the honesty and believability of the witnesses. These occurrences did not exist merely in the context of cleverly written stories, but real historical and personal circumstances. We are also told that remembrance of the words of Jesus were not left to chance, either, but that the Spirit would play a role in the memory of the apostles and in the memory of the church.

It is sad how much energy is expended in fighting polemic wars over the Bible rather than hearing it in a fresh way, the way a fifteen-year-old at a charismatic Bible study, led by Jesus freaks, once heard the Bible for the very first time.

My initial excitement with the Bible reminds me of what our Lord said about those who are best able to receive his revelations:

At that time Jesus answered and said, I thank thee, O Father, Lord of heaven and earth, because thou hast hid these things from the wise and prudent, and hast revealed them unto babes. (Matthew 11:25 KJV)

Let me reminisce again about my initial excitement about the Bible and my experience with my charismatic friends. It was the Holy Spirit's ministry to take my curiosity about the Bible and open my eyes to what was there for me to learn and personally feed upon as my spiritual food. It is the Holy Spirit who walked with this troubled pilgrim through good times and bad, providing comfort when needed or admonition when warranted, and the Holy Spirit has spoken through the scriptures.

For everything written in the past was written for our instruction, so that that through endurance and the encouragement of the Scriptures, we might have hope. (Romans 15:4 BSB).

What Is an Evangelical?

As a troubled Christian pilgrim, it bothers me that there's some misunderstanding about what the term *evangelical* means. Some associate the term with certain denominations, but the word itself goes beyond any denominational boundaries. It is a set of convictions about the nature of the Christian message. *Evangelical* is derived from the word *evangel,* an English derivative of the Greek word for *gospel.*

I would broadly define an evangelical as one who believes in the proclamation of the Gospel (or the evangel) based on the authority of the Word, a belief in the importance of repentance and personal faith, the sacrificial death and resurrection of Jesus, a view of the church grounded in the Apostles' Creed, a view of the Trinity grounded in the creed of Nicaea, a Christology grounded in the Council of Chalcedon, and an understanding of grace and salvation grounded in the teachings of the Protestant reformers. In the seventeenth and eighteenth centuries, the emphasis upon biblical devotion was expanded upon by groups like the Puritans and the Pietists.[34]

I would distinguish an evangelical from a Roman Catholic or an orthodox Christian in that salvation is wholly imparted by faith alone. These other church bodies tend to see salvation as a process, whereby through partaking of the sacraments and other graces of the church, we are redeemed over time, and if we fail to become fully redeemed, well, at least in the Roman view, there is always purgatory. The Roman Catholic Communion also tends to place the teachings of Catholic theologians, the magisterium or governing body of the church, and the pronouncements of the pope on the same authoritative level as apostolic scripture.[35]

In short, an evangelical is a Reformation Catholic, or as the term *Protestant* originally meant, a protesting Catholic. Catholic, you say? I thought that was the church with a pope and its own city-state? The term *catholic* predates the Roman church and has to do with the universality of the church and that it is Christ who called it into being and who recognizes who are truly his own in all Christian communions.

I would recite the Apostles' Creed in the churches I grew up in, and every time I did, I affirmed with others that there was "only one catholic and apostolic church."[36] The Lord and the apostles called the church into existence, and no one else. Jesus is the divider of the sheep and the goats, so to speak, and in all honesty, it is quite possible for sheep animals and goat animals to share the same pew. Jesus called this church into existence, which later manifested itself in the ecclesiastical bodies started by people.

The Reformation was based on Luther's five Latin Solas: Sola Gratia ("by grace alone"), Sola Fida ("by faith alone"), Sola Christus ("by Christ alone"), Sola Scriptura ("by scripture alone,"), and Sola Gloria ("for God's glory alone").[37] The three main reformers of Martin Luther, John Calvin, and Huldrych Zwingli were in basic agreement on these points, although Luther and Calvin differed from Zwingli on the issue of baptism and the Lord's supper.

The Roman church had taught the doctrine of transubstantiation, whereby the priest through consecration of the elements would cause the wine and the bread to literally become the body and blood of Jesus. Roman theologians used a distinction between reality and perception, developed by the Greek philosopher Aristotle, in describing what the bread and wine had become, versus the way those elements continued to be physically perceived. Calvin and Luther also believed in the sacramental significance of the Lord's supper, whereby a special grace of God was communicated and experienced. Luther saw the body and blood becoming real, as the believer partook of the sacrament, and Calvin envisioned rays of grace permeating the elements.

Zwingli viewed them as ordinances. Zwingli believed in the memorial view or remembrance view of the Lord's supper, and he also believed that the New Testament promoted infant baptism, although he believed in baptism as a sign of God's inward grace. He saw baptism as primarily a covenant action between parents and child before God.

However, Zwingli's view of baptism as a sign instead of a sacrament would influence the views of Anabaptists and others who began to practice believer's baptism instead, based on their reading of the New Testament. Whereas the Roman church viewed infant baptism as a sacrament that washed away original sin, the Reformers tended to see it as a symbol of God's grace coming to us before we are able to respond to it in faith, or in the case of Anabaptists and Baptists, both an acknowledgment of that grace and the Christian response to it.[38]

Some people call the Reformation an Augustinian revival, influenced by the theology of Saint Augustine, the greatest Christian thinker in church history, who lived in the fifth century. Luther was, after all, an Augustinian monk, and the theology of the reformers is largely a restatement of Augustine's theology, with some modifications.

I have been an evangelical since the age of sixteen, thanks in part to my education from the magazine *Christianity Today*. My basic convictions, as I defined above, have changed truly little in forty years, although my understanding of Jesus and the Trinity has deepened since that time, as well as my appreciation for the Bible, my understanding of the human condition, and the challenges of the Christian pilgrimage.

Many evangelicals deem themselves to be Bible Christians. They assert that they have no need for the creeds, which they view as high church vanity, and they also see no need to defer to the theology of the Protestant reformers, in their understanding of the major tenets of the faith. I accept the goodness and sincerity of such evangelical Christians, but I think they are mistaken.

Our understanding of the major doctrines of the Bible did not happen in a vacuum but reflects the traditions handed down to us. A good example of this would be the doctrine of the Jehovah's Witnesses that Jesus was an inferior creation of God, which is nothing more than a revival of the old Arian heresy that was put to rest at the Council of Nicaea in 325.[39]

Many assumptions that Bible Christians make about faith, the nature of God, and salvation reflect the legacy of the Protestant reformers and the ancient catholic or ecumenical creeds. After all, those who begin reading the Bible often embark on that task already expecting to find the divinity of Jesus, salvation, grace through faith alone, and the doctrine of the Trinity confirmed by their reading. They read their Bibles through the lens of what they were taught in their church and the tradition that informs that local body. Baptists, for instance, who generally shy away from ancient creeds, have a history full of confessions of faith and statements of belief that are essentially creeds in everything but name.

Grant you, many of the churches that have carried the traditions of the reformers have ossified into hallow shells of what they once were. However, our understanding of the deep mysteries of the Bible are not simply a matter of private interpretation. Our understanding of those mysteries reflects the thought and work of great minds dedicated to Christ.

I defer to the quadrilateral of Wesley: Our understanding of the faith reflects the quadrilateral of scripture, as interpreted through tradition, experience, and reason, illuminated by the Holy Spirit.[40] I believe that all Christians have the right to read and interpret the scriptures for themselves, and no interpretation is infallible. However, I also believe that some interpretations are better informed than others. How could it be any other way, if the Bible is to be trusted as a source of abiding and eternal truth?

A brief note: Bible Christians had a huge and positive influence on my walk with Christ. I only make this point to show that even the best of Christians can sometimes suffer from tunnel vision.

As a Reformation Catholic, I have been involved and associated with several denominations. Yet despite my participation in those ecclesiastical bodies, my basic theological convictions have remained the same. In all honesty, my convictions were better received in some bodies than in others, but my basic core identity has remained unchanged.

There are evangelicals present in practically all Christian bodies, the Unitarian church being the possible exception. The Roman church has found itself infected with evangelical and charismatic ideas that it has had a difficult time shaking off in recent decades, with ideas like parishioners reading the Bible for themselves and exercising spiritual gifts.

Many early reformers, like Englishman John Wycliffe (from the fourteenth century) and Bohemian (modern Czechoslovakia) John Huss (from the fifteenth century), were burned at the stake, for wanting common people to have access to the Bible in their native language. Common people having access to the Bible is also a hallmark of evangelical Catholicism. My first roommate at my seminary was a Moravian. The Moravians were part of the movement started by Huss in Czechoslovakia; their church predates the establishment of Protestantism. It was also at a Moravian meeting in London that John Wesley would have his famous heart-warming conversion.[41]

Some Orthodox and Roman communities have shown hostility to evangelicals, feeling threatened by a faith posture that emphasizes "the priesthood of all believers" and proclamation over the authority of any church communion. This is an area of disagreement between the great catholic bodies. The priesthood of all believers was emphasized by Martin Luther, who taught that Christian believers can directly access the graces of God without the assistance of an ordained priestly class to do it for them, thus making the church primarily a place of spiritual gathering and fellowship, instead of a mediator of grace and forgiveness.[42]

Evangelicals as a catholic group have a broad representation. There are evangelicals who are Calvinist (who believe in election and predestination), who are Arminian (who believe that grace is freely available to all), and Baptists, who are mix of the two. Charismatics are evangelicals. Most Pentecostals fall into the category of evangelicals, although some of them depart from Reformation catholic teaching, in their unorthodox understandings of the Trinity by baptizing new Christians in "Jesus's name only." Episcopalians are a mixed bag of liberals, sacramentalists, and evangelicals. This body has been dubbed by many, including their adherents, as Roman Catholic lite.

The Salvation Army, a holiness offshoot of Methodism founded by William Booth, is in the evangelical camp in its evangelistic endeavors, although this church body departs from reformation teaching in de-emphasizing the importance of the Lord's supper and baptism. However, the Army's social and humanitarian outreach is legendary and continues to touch my heart with its mission of compassion.[43]

The non-instrumental Churches of Christ could be considered evangelical with their revivals and outreach, although their insistence upon baptism as a prerequisite of salvation undercuts the reformation doctrine of salvation by faith alone and thus gave them the name of "water salvationists." The Churches of Christ were also an offshoot of the Disciples of Christ restoration movement, started by Alexander Campbell and Barton Stone.[44]

The Amish, Mennonites, and Dunkard Brethren represent unique Christian countercultures; they share many of the beliefs of evangelicals, although they undercut some of the salvation-by-faith-alone message by the imposition of a corporate discipline, not only for the sake of community membership but, by implication, one's possible standing before God.[45]

Quakers, and their American patriarch William Penn, were an unusual group of Christians who emphasized the "inner light." The Quakers and their offshoot movement, the Shakers, have no formal clergy and conduct meetings waiting for the Spirit's direction. A socially conscious group in America, they worked against slavery, and like the Amish, many of them are pacifists and opposed to war. They were more grounded in experience than doctrine when compared with evangelicalism in general. However, there are also evangelical Quakers who emphasize proclamation of the Christian message. Presidents Herbert Hoover and Richard Nixon came out of this unique movement.[46]

Some Presbyterians, influenced by what I call hyper-Calvinism (a term I learned concerning primitive Baptists; if God wants them in church, he will send them there) or a tepid universalism, can come across as anti-evangelistic or indifferent to the call of repentance and personal faith. Baptists often chide Presbyterians as the "frozen chosen."[47]

Some tepid Presbyterians will chide anyone who emphasizes proclamation and conversion as wanting to be like the Baptists or Methodists, heaven forbid. Yet the most popular Christian witnessing tool in recent history, *Evangelism Explosion,* was authored by the late Presbyterian Calvinist D. James Kennedy of Coral Ridge Presbyterian Church in Fort Lauderdale, Florida. Therefore, being an evangelical is not a Baptist thing or a Methodist thing but an evangelical thing, period. Thus, in my opinion, evangelicalism is a position that most consistently emphasizes all the aspects of Reformation faith, regardless of denominational affiliation.

What Is a Fundamentalist?

Fundamentalism is the most conservative branch of evangelicalism. In the 1970s, my mom would stay up late and watch Pastor Jerry Falwell and *The Old Time Gospel Hour.* My parents even thought of sending me to the school he had started at one point, which was ironic, considering where I later attended college.

For many people in the country, Jerry Falwell came to symbolize fundamentalism. Oddly enough, he tried to reform fundamentalism, de-emphasizing biblical separation and promoting the social and political activism of conservative Christians, in alliance with other religious groups.[48]

My wife grew up with old-style fundamentalism in Wisconsin, which emphasized authoritarian pastors and their absolute spiritual authority, and ignored ideas like the priesthood of all believers or lay ministry. The ministers preached salvation by grace alone (*sola gratis*) but practiced salvation by works, motivated by guilt. My wife would later attend the premier fundamentalist institution in America, Bob Jones University. It took her many years to recover from fundamentalism and embrace grace. Fundamentalism would also figure into the controversy at my seminary in relation to pastoral authority.

Yet little did anyone in my family suspect we would move right into Falwell's backyard in central Virginia. My father's departure from a very prominent job with a hospital supply company in Florida propelled us to the central Virginia area.

I can tell you that being in the shadow of Falwell taught me much about the power of the fundamentalist movement. I also learned about the prejudice against it from the intellectual and social elites, some of whom were well represented at my alma mater. My school prided itself on being avant-garde and open to new ideas, unless they came from Falwell. Professors from my school jointly wrote a satirical book about Falwell that was more persnickety than funny. A good book to read about Falwell and Lynchburg is *Falwell before the Millennium* by Dinesh D'Souza.

My college was associated with the company my dad went to work for. We joined a mainline church in the central Virginia area that was affiliated with my college; some of the professors were members of the congregation. There were about three hundred churches in a community of some hundred thousand people, along with several colleges, in an area the size of Washington DC.

I was a townie student and did not make too many social connections. However, I became acquainted with a college professor who was also a clergyman, and I took an Old Testament survey course under him. This is when I first learned about Dr. Harold Kushner's book *When Bad Things Happen to Good People*, and the book that would change my life, *The Wounded Healer,* by Henri

Nouwen. Later, I would develop some friendships through the campus chapter of Yokefellow Mission Group, started nationally by D. Elton Trueblood, a Quaker theologian and scholar.[49]

Lynchburg was an important town in the Civil War. General Jubal Early fooled the invading Yankees by moving empty train cars, presumably filled with rebels, pulled by a locomotive. The rebel soldiers never actually moved. They all remained stationed in one place.[50] In the conflict's final battle, General Ulysses S. Grant trapped Robert E. Lee's Army of Northern Virginia between Lynchburg and Appomattox, prompting Lee's surrender in 1865. It is a town rich in history and religious affiliation.[51]

Yet the favorite topic of conversation was Jerry Falwell and what he was doing in, for, and to the community. In 1983, my older brother and I went to hear Senator Ted Kennedy speak at Liberty College. Falwell relished using such occasions to irritate the cultured elites of the town. More recently, in 2018, President Jimmy Carter addressed Liberty's graduating class.[52]

During that time, I lived in the same town as Falwell and also subscribed to his magazine, *The Fundamentalist Journal.* All in all, it was a surprisingly good publication, which made it clear how fundamentalists were different from your average evangelical. Mainstream evangelicals were often the target of the magazine's ire, as Falwell would fume about the liberal trends in presumably conservative denominations. As an example, my wife was taught that Southern Baptists and other evangelicals were hopelessly liberal and headed for eternal damnation. Her church was a little less political than Falwell's.

This would only contribute to the irony of me becoming a student at a mainstream evangelical institution, or that fateful Sunday morning when a fellow student and I attended a service at Thomas Road Baptist Church; we went up afterward to shake Falwell's hand. When my friend mentioned the institution we attended, Falwell gave us a very pained and disgruntled smile.

When my dad heard about that visit, he concluded that Falwell was afraid of my seminary.

Fundamentalism was crystalized at the Niagara Conference, held in 1878 in Niagara Falls, New York. The conference produced a set of fourteen points that most fundamentalists would agree with, such as a belief in verbal inspiration, a literal Bible interpretation, and the pre-millennial second coming of Jesus.[53]

Fundamentalism was solidified in the early twentieth century with the publication of *The Fundamentals: A Testimony to the Truth.* It was a set of ninety essays published between 1910 and 1915 by the Testimony Publishing Co. of Chicago. The Bible Institute of Los Angeles, now known as Biola, was involved in the publication, which attacked modernism, various religious cults, evolution, and higher criticism. It became a twelve-volume set with contributors like James Orr, Benjamin Warfield, R. A. Torrey, and even Southern Baptist theologian E. Y. Mullins.

Lyman Stewart, a California businessman, founder of Union Oil, and a devout Presbyterian and dispensationalist, originally had the idea for *The Fundamentals* back in 1909 and provided the funds for their publication. Fundamentalist bodies tend to be loose fellowships of cooperating, independently operated churches; fundamentalists are also present in regular church denominations.[54]

Billy Sunday, a baseball player from Chicago and a convert at the Pacific Garden Mission, was a great Presbyterian fundamentalist and evangelist from the late nineteenth century to the mid-1930s. One of the women's dormitories at Bob Jones University is named after his wife, Nell. I remember seeing his picture at the Pacific mission when a fellow student and I visited the mission in 1987. I had partnered with him to do church planting work as part of a practicum course, out of my seminary, in cooperation with the denomination's mission outreach.

Billy Sunday had a summer home in Winona Lake, Indiana, where my father was born. He would invite residents to participate in services led by Homer Rodeheaver (an auditorium at Bob Jones University is named for him). After Sunday's death in 1935, his widow, Nell, or "Ma Sunday," as my dad and relatives used to call her, would continue Billy's tradition, including wearing huge diamond rings and garish jewelry (sort of a sign of things to come with the lifestyles of evangelistic empires).

In the early to mid-1990s, I ran around with a rat pack of students who attended the Liberty Bible Institute (LBI), which was a non-accredited branch of Falwell's university. I also worked as a security guard at a local bank in Central Virginia with some of the LBI students. I attended a class, a chapel service at Liberty, and heard W. A. Criswell and Adrian Rogers speak on the LBI campus. One Liberty Bible Institute professor I heard said that he was "so pre-millennial that he could not eat Post Toasties cereal."

I also became acquainted with the ugly attitudes toward my alma mater and its "liberal" professors. I often heard Liberty students, even one I made friends with, run down my school, which angered and insulted me. I realized that as conservative as I might have considered myself, I was not a fundamentalist, and fundamentalists would probably not claim me, either, regardless of how much respect I may have shown their ministry.

They tend to view anyone outside the fundamentalist fold, including other evangelicals, as part of the apostate church, which must be rejected; my wife felt this way when she was in the fundamentalist fold. This separation of the body of Christ troubled me. As my beloved preaching professor once said, "Fundamentalists can be mean." The truth of that statement always made me feel sad.

By the mid-1990s, my own identity had solidified further, as I came to realize that as an evangelical and Reformation Catholic, I had a growing distaste for excessive judgmentalism and ecclesiastical provincialism. I happen to respect all bodies of Christianity that have contributed to the Christian tradition in general, evangelical Christianity, in particular.

What I did not like was for any branch to claim primacy or superiority over another. I support the great works of the Kingdom of God that happen in the various Christian communions, all over the world, when in fact those works happen. I am quite confident that if God can "raise up stones to be children of Abraham"

(Matthew 3:9 ESV), then everyone can be used to advance the work of the Kingdom, if they are willing.

For me to be an evangelical Catholic is to be a catholic in a very authentic sense of the word. It is to be generous person, who can work alongside any Christian, and sometimes those of other faiths, if the values of the kingdom are being served.

Are Catholic and Roman Catholic Synonymous?

What did the Roman church have to do with the two most significant creeds in Christian history: Nicaea and Chalcedon? From what I can tell, nothing. If anything, the Orthodox Church communities have the most direct link to these ancient Catholic confessions of any group. I also affirm those creeds as a Protestant, which means a protesting Catholic.

Over the centuries, the Roman church has made an audacious claim, asserting its apostolic primacy over the Orthodox church and the Protestants. They assert that Peter was the first pope and founder of the Roman church. Yet is there anything historical to support the idea of Peter as the first pope or vicar of Christ, as the office is called? In fact, if there was an original bishop of the church, it was James, the brother of Jesus. This is what is asserted in the New Testament book of Acts. James was the titular head of the church in Jerusalem. Peter and John constituted his spiritual council or small magisterium, so to speak.

Peter's significant role would be his sermon at Pentecost, as a spiritual advisor to James and in supporting Paul's idea of lifting of Torah observance for new Gentile converts at the Council of Jerusalem, as recorded in Acts. Peter would be "the rock upon which Christ would build his church," and the name Peter means "rock" (Matthew 16:18 NLT). However, Peter's role would mainly be a supportive one and not a pontifical one, it would appear.

Peter's spiritual power in being given the keys to the Kingdom by Christ was present in his persuasive role as a preacher, as an advisor to James, and as Paul's advocate at the Council of Jerusalem. Peter would also be martyred on an upside-down cross in Rome, no doubt cementing his ties with the church in Rome. Yet James, the original spiritual leader of the church, had no ties with Rome.

We tend to revere Paul as the premier Christian apostle who castigated the "Judaizers" in the book of Galatians; the Judaizers insisted that gentile Christians observe the Jewish law. Yet the so-called Judaizers were, at the time, the official representatives of the church in Jerusalem, of whom James was the spiritual leader. Paul was the radical, who was undermining the official authority of Bishop James and the Jerusalem church. Paul is a hero, but only in the hindsight of subsequent church history. After all, Paul was not among the original apostles who personally knew Jesus. Paul spent his early career as an open enemy to the church and claimed apostolic authority on an entirely mystical basis.

Many contemporary folks, including many Christians, have mixed feelings about Paul. He has been viewed as everything from a tyrant to a hero. A conservative rabbi in a ministerial association I attended once told me, "Robert, we are okay with Jesus; it is Paul we have a problem with."

I once invited a Messianic Jew, a Jew who believes in Jesus as the messiah, who was president of a ministerial association, to address the member clergy. A group of rabbis came to the meeting to confront him. This was an uncomfortable and tense moment for me. I did feel sorry for my guest. However, what stood out in my memory of that meeting was being confronted by the community relations director for the local Jewish Federation, who shared with me that Christianity had cut its ties with Judaism at the Council of Jerusalem. This was the council where James, the official leader of the church, famously compromised with Paul, in rescinding the requirement that new Gentile converts observe the Jewish law (with the exception of not eating meat strangled in its own blood or meat that was dedicated to idols).

Paul's leadership led to Christianity becoming its own distinct faith, apart from Judaism. This change is exemplified by the phrase from Galatians 3:28 (ESV), "There is neither Jew nor Greek, there is neither slave nor free, there is no male and female, for you are all were one in Christ Jesus." Paul, for good or ill, launched the Christian faith that we know. The director of the Jewish Federation was quick to quote the above passage of Galatians to me.[55]

Ironically, Martin Luther would later play the role of Paul, in confronting the medieval Roman church with its own forms of overbearing legalisms. Luther, formerly a member of an Augustinian Catholic order, was looking to reform the Roman church and not create a schism, but that was not to be. Luther's passionate pleas at the council known as the Diet of Worms fell on hostile ears. There would be no reconciliation like at the Council of Jerusalem, and no one was probably more disappointed by that than Luther himself.[56]

Paul could have seen himself as the new bishop of the church, but it doesn't appear that he ever viewed himself that way. He saw his apostleship as a unique gift of grace and a prophetic calling. I don't say this to disparage the Roman Catholic Church but to argue that its faith grew out of the Catholicism of the larger Christian world and from orthodox confessions. Oddly enough, what can be argued is that the Roman Catholic Church took the model of the old Holy Roman empire in structuring its government.

After the decline of the original Roman empire, a new one emerged, with Constantine as its leader. He saw a cross in a vision and heard a voice that told him, "In this symbol conquer." Constantine officially ended the persecution of the Christians; in fact, he converted to the Roman church and made Christianity the new official religion of the empire.

Constantine's mother Helena collected artifacts from the Holy Land, including an alleged piece of the cross of Jesus, and identified all the major holy sites we now visit there. She ordered the building of a church at the birth site of Jesus in Bethlehem. She ordered a church built on the site of the Ascension on the Mount of Olives. She also uncovered the tomb of Jesus, which had a temple to either Jupiter or Venus built over it (a subject of speculation). The Roman

Emperor Hadrian had this temple built around AD 130, as his way of desecrating the site. Constantine himself ordered a church built over that site.

Constantine was both the secular ruler and the self-appointed head of Christianity in the empire, which included the Roman communion and Orthodox bodies. In 316, in the Edict of Milan, Constantine granted amnesty to Christians who renounced their faith during the Roman persecution.

In 325, Constantine called a council in the Greek city of Nicaea (which is now part of Turkey) and appointed Bishop Athanasius to convene Christian bishops from around the world to settle a controversy about the nature of the divine Trinity, particularly as it related to Jesus. The creed that came out of this first ecumenical council became the single most important theological statement in Christian history.

In 330, he moved the capital of the Roman empire to the city of Byzantium in Turkey, renaming it Constantinople, thus making Constantinople the center of the ancient Christian world, *not* Rome. Constantine and Helena are considered Christian saints in the Orthodox communities.[57]

The Holy See of Rome broke away from the Holy Roman empire's authority and combined the roles of Constantine and Athanasius into one titular church head under its civil leader, who was officially named Pontifex Maximus; it later created its own holy state, modelled in part on the Holy Roman empire.

The Roman church became a sovereign church state that functioned alongside, but independently of, civil rulers and monarchs. As the old Eastern empire collapsed, it became increasingly difficult to maintain unity in the church. Thus, in 1054, the Roman church and the Orthodox community split.[58]

A few years ago, I attended a panel discussion of orthodox clergy held at a Princeton seminary. They did an excellent job of articulating the fact that orthodox communities, like the Greek Orthodox church, began with the planting of churches in Greece in the first century, thus predating the founding of the Roman church (or at least occurring around the same time). Churches were established at about the same time in Turkey, Egypt, Ethiopia, and other parts of the world, with their own bishops and orthodox communities.

One can hardly imagine the suffering that the Armenian Orthodox community suffered under the Turks over the centuries, particularly at the time of World War I, when over a million and a half Armenian Christians were systematically murdered by the Turkish government. The fact that Constantinople, which was renamed by the Muslim Turks as the modern-day city of Istanbul, an Islamic stronghold, was once the capital of a Christian empire and the center of the Christian world is a truly tragic fact of history.

The Council of Nicaea was convened in Turkey. Saint Paul himself was born in Tarsus, Turkey. The magnificent churches of what was once Constantinople were converted into mosques, with their Christian art covered over, as my wife attested after coming back from a mission trip she took to Istanbul.

I spent the first several years of my life reciting in church the Apostle's Creed, also known as the Roman Creed, from the third century AD, acknowledging the "one holy catholic church." This holy catholic church is comprised of all believers in Jesus, particularly the ones who believe in the historic tenets of the Christian faith.

This would include the Roman church, the Orthodox churches, and the traditional Protestants. We may not agree on everything, particularly concerning our views of faith and sacrament, but in terms of our acceptance of the great catholic and ecumenical confessions, our faith rests on the same foundation.

I have no desire to upset my Roman Catholic friends and family members, but it has always troubled me that the Roman Catholic church has misled its followers about its actual origins, thus making boasts about their connection to Peter, or even asserting the idea that Peter was the first bishop or pope, when such an assertion had no historical or biblical basis. James was the original head of the church in Jerusalem. Peter never acted as the official head of the church. Peter always submitted to the authority of James as the official head of the church.

Peter and Paul worked together as equals in service to Christ and the Jerusalem church. Peter may have played a role in establishing and nurturing the church in Rome, but then, so did Paul, whose greatest theological treatise was his letter written to the Romans. Paul was also martyred in Rome.

Paul established congregations in Greece and Turkey, where the original orthodox churches developed their belief and practices. The direct ties that the Orthodox communities had to the apostle Paul were as strong as, if not stronger than, that of Rome. The ties of the Orthodox communities to the greatest of ecumenical or catholic creeds were even more so. The Council of Chalcedon, concerning the two natures of Christ, was the third great ecumenical council; it was convened around 451 by the Holy Roman Emperor Marcian, in what is now modern Kadikoy, Turkey.[59] Nine of Paul's letters were addressed to churches in Greece. Therefore, the Roman church is not, nor has it ever been, the sole representative of the catholic faith.

Could it be argued that the Roman church merely appropriated Peter as their symbolic founder or first pontiff? Possibly. Just as I would argue that John the Baptist symbolically assumed the mantle of Elijah, and Paul did the same with Abraham. The popes could see themselves as taking on the mantle of Peter. I see no problem with that and would applaud the issue being put in that context. However, they could have just as easily assumed the mantle of James, in a symbolic sense as well.

Yet I have never perceived it as expressed that way. Apostolic succession or an organic connection of an unbroken chain of Catholic vicars, starting with the apostle Peter, is what has been promulgated. A very literal connection with Peter is what is generally implied, and that is what the facts of church history (and the biblical record, in my opinion) would dispute.

You might wonder why I appear to be obsessed over this one issue. Why make such a big deal over this? Shouldn't we be past such arcane debates in our postmodern world? There is a reason for my rant. The claims of the Roman church being the epicenter of global Catholic faith is predicated on its apostolic primacy, a primacy that it asserts itself above all other churches, who otherwise share in the catholic faith of the apostles.

It is not the Roman church's catholic witness that I challenge, or its positive contributions, but only its exclusive and grandiose claims compelling the church at large to treat all other Christian communions as its inferior. This same view still compels some within its communion to believe that there is no salvation or grace outside of the Roman church.

My opinions here do not negate my general respect for the Roman church; I am expressing something that has troubled me, and so I proffer this perspective. Bear in mind, this is the same church that would not allow me to participate in their sacrament, and only recently have they recognized non-Roman baptisms. When I was ministerial association president, I recall meeting a new Roman Catholic bishop from the local diocese. I introduced myself and my denomination; the bishop replied by saying, "So that is your denomination; I am aware of their corrupt morals."

I do admit, I did participate in a Mass at a friend's church, but only because the priest was unaware that I was a Protestant. I also acknowledge the right of the Roman church, and all communities of faith, to establish their own boundaries of inclusion and exclusion. I am only offering my opinion, and it is one bound to be controversial, but one that is rooted in conviction.

A few years ago, I even had the honor of an audience with Pope John Paul II, with a group of Lutheran clergy, at the papal auditorium in Rome, under the auspices of a local diocese. We all shouted, "Viva la Papa," as the Italians there did, in honor of John Paul II, whose moral and political courage, particularly as it related to Soviet Communism, I personally admired.

In 1983, John Paul II also took a significant step in ecumenical relations, by going to Wittenberg, Germany, on the five hundredth anniversary of Martin Luther's birthday, acknowledging Luther's positive contributions to church reform. This was an incredibly significant turning point in history.[60] The Roman church has had several reforms in this century, most notably, Vatican II. Perhaps in the wake of the COVID-19 crisis, and the practical challenges that this poses for the Roman church, the reform that Luther sought to bring about in the Roman church in his time will finally come to fruition in our own time.

I continue to admire the courage of the Roman Catholic church in speaking out for the sanctity of life, the charitable work of the Roman church's spiritual orders, and its insistence on decency in our culture and entertainment. I also respect the intellectual tradition of St. Thomas Aquinas and the faith examples of St. Francis, Thomas Merton, and the late Henri Nouwen. The contributions of the Roman church to Western culture, art, architecture, and science is huge.

I am a Reformation Catholic, but I share many of the same values and beliefs that characterize my Roman brothers and sisters, as well as my Orthodox ones. I hope that someday, we will be united in spirit, as well as in moral and intellectual convictions, despite our differences, acknowledging our common catholic faith.

The New Testament Church was distinct and separate from any church that came after it, although it inspired the planting of new communities across the known Western world. Paul and others made that their mission. Paul's execution in Rome cemented his ties with the capital city. Paul, who never sought to be a bishop, was emulated because of his celibacy by the Roman church, even though he claimed that his celibacy was a gift but not an obligation to those who would serve Christ. Peter, the first pope in the Roman view, was married. As Paul himself expressed, "I wish that all were as I myself am. But each has his own gift from God, one of one kind and one of another" (1 Corinthians 7:7 ESV).

As a troubled pilgrim, I have no desire to upset my Roman Catholic brothers and sisters any more than my Protestant ones, because many of them are awesome Christians and have prayed for and supported me, but truth is what our faith should be about. Historical truth should matter, even regarding religion.

Chapter 4

THE MODERN CHURCH STRUGGLES AND CONTROVERSIES

Bread and Circuses, Anyone?

I was not an athletic kid; I was uncoordinated, hyperactive, and bookish. My older brother was athletic. My sister was a great softball player, and my brother excelled in track and wrestling. In fact, he was so good at wrestling that he had to quit the intramural team out of fear he might harm someone. He was lightning fast, as well, which was why I never did well in any fight I had with him, although he was good at beating up neighborhood bullies on my behalf. I was the last to be picked for sports teams in school and frequently assisted in the losing of sports games. Well, you get the idea. At this point, you may be able to hear the violins playing.

However, our family, living in South Florida, loved to watch the Dolphins play at the Orange Bowl. I sort of liked it, but I mainly looked forward to the popcorn and refreshments. At that time, you could buy a whole season of tickets for a reasonable price, and football players were generally good people you could look up to and emulate. Our teacher in elementary school even had quarterback Bob Griese come speak to us about the importance of hard work and perseverance. We are just talking the 1970s, folks.

What a difference a few decades make. Now, the average fan can hardly afford to go to a professional game without emptying their bank account. The players, who makes bundles of money, can be anything from felons with assault charges to people who gamble on illegal dog fights. Yet we are still supposed to admire them for their athletic prowess and their ability to score points for our favorite team.

At the 2020 Super Bowl, the halftime show presented dances and gyrations that were openly sexually explicit and near pornographic. I complained to someone on Facebook about this issue, and he replied, "People can always change the channel." I retorted that "this was not the adult channel, but the biggest live show presented on television." My acquaintance was unmoved, and I was saddened by how the morals of our culture were beginning to sink.

Couple examples like this with the availability of every kind of salacious entertainment, and you have contemporary America. What are we saying as a society with all of this? Well, if I didn't know any better, I would say it would be to numb our moral sensibilities and forget that we are witnessing the decline of our own civilization. There was, after all, an empire in ancient times that went through a similar phase.

That being the late, great Roman empire, which crumbled politically, economically, and morally, but managed to keep the masses in check with grotesque burlesque entertainment and violent gladiator fights. Ironically, a show came out a few years ago entitled, and yes you have probably guessed it, *American Gladiators*. Sports are less about sportsmanship and more about bloodthirst these days, as we relish watching fights and injuries. It has become about greed as well, as sports franchises gladly increase ticket prices to cash in on the fans' lust for more.

Oddly enough, with the Kaepernick controversy, football has taken a financial hit, because many fans discovered that they loved their country as much as, if not more than, they did football. I am making no judgment here about the Kaepernick affair, which I think is a complex one. By kneeling during the national anthem, he was seeking to call attention to police brutality in the African American community, a sentiment that I can understand, although he doesn't have much good to say about America in general, from what I read in news reports. I am deeply disappointed in America too, but I don't express that dismay by praising third world despots. Kaepernick has.[61]

Which gets to my deeper point: America has had its senses so dulled by the arena and bread and circuses, is it any wonder that we struggle to solve our most pressing social problems? Solving those problems requires a public that not only is engaged but also has a strong sense of right and wrong.

Don't misunderstand me; I enjoy watching sports and love to be entertained, but there is a point at which one can be entertained to death. Many Americans seem to have reached that low point in their existence. We go see movies that are produced by people who hate Christian values but who rail against the greed of capitalism in America.

Yet is there is an industry that exemplifies greed more than Hollywood? Let me ask you a question: Have you ever wondered about the outrageous price gouging you experience at an average movie theater concession? Do you know why that is? Because as any theater owner will tell you, that is where most of their profits come from, certainly not from movie ticket sales.

Here we have a global film industry that makes billions in profits, and their distribution network of theaters are forced to raise the price of popcorn just to make a profit. Can you imagine any other industry in America where the share of profits within their distribution network is that appallingly low?

There is a name for that. It is called greed. Now local chains are even upselling their regular customers by offering better sound and 3-D experiences, at a higher cost; that is a little bit greedy too, but who can blame them? However, at the time of my writing, theaters have been forced to close because of the COVID-19 scare. Who knows what the final economic impact of this situation will be? Perhaps by the time you read this, a clear picture will emerge.

So forgive me if I am irritated by movie stars or sport celebrities lecturing to us about morals while robbing customers and even business partners, just to put more money in their pockets, while dulling our moral senses about the world. Even before Kaepernick came on the scene, I was hoping that sports fans would have the hutzpah to boycott games, or moviegoers would stop going to see films, till they put out a more uplifting product or changed the way they did business.

I will say that my wife and I did start attending minor league games a few years ago and loved it. Reasonable ticket prices, players in it for the love of the game, and a family-friendly environment. I highly recommend the experience. We still attend the movies but frequent the library and video store more for our entertainment. Perhaps we can do more of that, and so can you, even after the economy fully reopens, and we will all see what emerges, by God's grace.

Am I dreaming? Probably. However, in Proverbs 29:18 (KJV), we read, "Where there is no vision, the people perish." As a troubled Christian pilgrim, if I had a prayer, it would be that more people of faith would reclaim a vision of what a wholesome society should at least look like. Then we could work together to reclaim the culture from the abyss it has sunk into. Is it too late to do anything about this? It might be, but what would it hurt to try? Christ went to the cross for the sinfulness of the world; the least we can do is open our mouths and close our wallets.

When Life Begins Is the Wrong Question

On January 22, 1973, when the *Roe versus Wade* decision was authorized by the Supreme Court, I was nine years old. My own life was unaffected by this court case, and I had no reason to think about it. I was too busy thinking about UFOs, *The Planet of the Apes*, and my favorite comic book characters.

Yet the world I grew up in would be profoundly changed by it. Abortion, which had been a relatively restricted procedure, varying from state to state, was now available upon demand as a legal, social, and medical right.

The case was complex but revolved around a plaintiff, Norma McCorvey, dubbed *Jane Doe* in the case, who had lived a very rough, rebellious, and promiscuous life in east Texas. Attending reform school, she also had sex with the other girls. She had already put up some children for adoption. In 1970, all she wanted was an abortion, which she was having a difficult time obtaining under Texas law. She would eventually have the baby in question and put it up for adoption. Attorneys like Gloria Allred became involved with the case, and Norma found herself swept up in events that she would later regret.

Norma ran a cleaning business and continued to be celebrated for her role in the famous case. However, she herself had remorse over what had transpired in the country as a result of the decision. She became a Christian and was baptized in the mid-1990s. She became a prolife activist and angered many who had used her as a pawn in this volatile issue.[62]

The same year Norma was seeking an abortion, my mother became pregnant with my younger brother. It was an unplanned pregnancy. My mother had health conditions that would be exacerbated by the pregnancy, and my mother's gynecologist recommended that she consider having an abortion. This was in Tennessee, which like other states had restrictions on abortion, but medical reasons were allowed as a legitimate warrant for it. Ultimately, my parents opted to have my brother, and he was born on December 8, 1970.

Before you get your defenses up, allow me to state that I am not an absolutist on this issue. I think it is a gut-wrenching and complex issue that involves every human factor imaginable. I know women who have had abortions, and I understand that a lot went into their decisions. I kept those decisions in confidence because of respect for their privacy and the moral angst surrounding the decisions. I am also in favor of contraception and birth control. Another reason to be Protestant (yes, I am being sarcastic).

I do object to the assertions that comes out of organizations like Planned Parenthood that there were no safe abortions prior to the 1973 decision. There were many legal and safe abortions happening in the twenty states that allowed for abortions, within their legal criteria. Deaths did occur from botched abortions, but the number was relatively low. Again, I am troubled by people who advance their cause through a one-sided historical narrative.[63]

I also object to the never-ending (and pointless) debates about when life begins. Somehow, the whole issue of life has come down to something as elusive as how many angels can sit on the head of a pin. A friend and counselor of mine, who happens to be a vegetarian, has shared with me about the value of all creatures God endowed with the gift of life. While I am still a carnivore, this observation has made an impression.

I am more likely now to think about the fact that the life of a cow, pig, or lamb, for instance, was sacrificed so I could enjoy my pleasant repast. I recall a ritual that used to be done by native Americans, who immediately after killing a deer or buffalo would thank the animal for offering its life in the service of their lives and then would dedicate the spirit of the animal to the Great Spirit.

What does this have to do with the topic at hand? I have come to understand the preciousness of all life. I even find myself wincing at having to flush a cockroach down the toilet; I find myself tossing them out the door on occasion. I find no enjoyment in the idea of killing.

So am I in sympathy with those who want to preserve certain species in nature? Yes. Yet, if all that God has created is a precious part of his creation, then how much more precious is the life of humanity, when it was created specifically in God's image? This is where I am troubled by a huge disconnect in our larger culture and world. While I dislike the abuse and wanton destruction of animals, how many people even think about the untold number of children who are the victims of abuse and wanton destruction?

What matters is not when human life begins, but whether it has any intrinsic value at all. Who assigns the value of a given life, anyway? Did my life have more intrinsic value at ten than it did when I was an infant? Am I a more valuable creature at my current age than I was at twenty-six? Based on what criteria? I could argue that I have more in the wisdom department, although it's doubtful that I would have more value in the physical department.

The reality is that at each stage, I was on a journey, a pilgrimage, on my way to becoming the person I am today and will be in the future. People who die at a young age, or as children, are robbed of that journey toward the person they could have become.

The utilitarian ethic is predominating the world right now. We look at people like they are things. Are they productive? Are they useful? Are they a burden? Can we do without them? Have they become obsolete? Some countries are now encouraging the abortion of Down syndrome babies. For example, 100 percent of babies determined to have Down Syndrome in Iceland are aborted, 98 percent in Denmark, 77 percent in France, and 67 percent in the United States.[64]

Our older population is being viewed this way in terms of health care costs. Why can't we just keep them comfortable so they can die in peace? Some are even talking seriously about human flesh as an acceptable meat source, as appalling as that sounds. We live in a time where some in the world are openly supportive of cannibalism. A behavioral scientist from Sweden named Magnus Soderlund has advocated eating people to save the planet and its resources.[65]

Have you ever seen the movie *Soylent Green*? The film, starring Charlton Heston and Edward G. Robinson, envisioned a future where natural resources became scare but there was a synthetic food source, called soylent green, that keep the populace fed. Heston plays a police investigator who is trying to find out how the dead are actually disposed of by the corporation that is in charge of managing waste and resources. At the end of the movie, he makes a shocking discovery, as he sees human bodies travelling on a factory belt, and soylent green coming out the other end. He screams at the top of his lungs, "Soylent green is people! Soylent green is people."

When that movie came out in the early 1970s, few people could imagine that kind of future, but we can. We live in a present where Planned Parenthood has admitted that it sold the parts of babies for profit. We live in a time where a Virginia governor advocated for infanticide and a New York governor signed into law a late-term abortion bill that was met with applause. Currently, nine states allow abortion up to birth.[66] Whatever became of the position of President Bill Clinton that abortions should be "safe, legal, and rare"? Such rhetoric seems to no longer be popular in liberal, prochoice circles.

One of the ironies of the forced abortion policy in China is a shortage of women.[67] Even more ironic is that Christianity is bigger in China than in the United States. Odd, how when the ship of a corrupt culture really starts to sink, the heart and minds of the populace become more open to a divine life raft.

Prochoice women say men should have no say about abortion because it is not their body. However, what is often overlooked in this whole discussion are the ways promiscuous men have benefited from the availability of abortion. It is often boyfriends who are the ones pressuring their girlfriends to get rid of the baby. Promiscuous men see abortion as an easy way out of becoming a father, with the legal and financial obligations that such a circumstance can incur.

Being prolife is only in the interest of men who think babies should be cared for, cherished, and raised by both men and women. Being prolife is broader than caring about unborn and born children. Jim Wallis of the Sojourners, who I don't always agree with, made this astute observation: "For prochoice people, concern for life begins at birth, and for prolife people, it tends to end there."

Yet it is beginning to appear that even birth may not be a guarantee of protection for babies, as infanticide is being seriously discussed. Many think that abortion is the sign of a civilized society. Were the abortions that ancient Romans forced upon women a sign of a civilized society? Were the numerous abortions that occurred after the devastation of the American Civil War a positive sign of anything? Is the forced abortion policy of China a humane position?

Abortion is a symptom of a society that has given up, at least for a time, on the virtues of family, chastity, and caring. Abortion itself is not the problem. It is a procedure that is sometimes warranted, although not usually desirable and sad when it happens.

The explosion of abortions in America is a symptom, I believe, of a society that values career, success, and convenience more than it does human life. Simply restricting abortions is not the answer, either, if it only frustrates such intentions. Cherishing life for its own sake is the real answer, I believe: cherishing life across the spectrum, caring about the preciousness of life from birth to death.

The abortion tragedy is at least as much a collective sin as it is an individual one. Our indifference to the issue of single mothers has contributed as much to the problem as anything else. Financially supporting or otherwise helping both mothers and children is what shows a sincere prolife commitment. There are many such endeavors out there, although they are primarily of a religious affiliation.

Many people point out that abortion clinics are disproportionally present in minority communities. I would argue that the population growth of African Americans has been significantly lower than any other group in America, in part, because of the high abortion rate in that community. The Guttmacher Institute recently claimed that "black women are more than five times as likely as white women to have an abortion." This is a tragic story all its own.[68]

As someone who works in special needs, I know firsthand

the gift that every human life can be. God speaks through broken people and shows me how he can love me in my brokenness. Each life can be its own unique stained-glass window, with the light of Christ shining through each special creation.

You might be wondering at this point about my opinion concerning women who have had abortions. Honestly, I feel compassion. Unless you have no normal emotions, abortion is likely to leave a lasting scar on your life, even if you have strong prochoice convictions.

I have come to my own strong belief about the love of Christ. It is that nothing can defeat it. Nothing can defeat Christ's purpose for those he loves. Human mistakes, human evil, and even the cruelty of nature cannot defeat Christ's victory over death. As it is written in Romans:

> Who shall separate us from the love of Christ? Shall tribulation, or distress, or persecution, or famine, or nakedness, or peril, or sword? As it is written, for thy sake we are killed, all the day long; we are accounted as sheep for the slaughter. Nay, in all these things we are more than conquerors through him that loved us. (Romans 8:35–37 KJV)

We can mourn for a miscarriage, an infant lost from crib death, or a child who dies from a choking, like one of my grandnephews did recently at the age of four. We can mourn that we will never know them, that they were denied the privilege of this life with its joys, sorrows, and challenges.

Yet what we can know is that Jesus has a special place in his heart for the little ones. While they may have been denied this life, with its joys, challenges, and sorrows, they are experiencing the everlasting joy of being with the Lord Jesus as children forever. This is equally true of the little ones who died from war, pestilence, starvation, and disease.

The souls of countless children made in God's image are

living in his presence as we speak. Little children from places like Auschwitz, Rwanda, the Sudan, Serbia, China, Russia, Iran, Israel, Palestine, and many other places. As the hymn goes, "Jesus loves the little children of the world. Yellow, black and white, they are precious in his sight."

Lastly, many of the women I knew who had abortions went on to have children. Is there a reason for them or anyone else to feel sadness? No, our Lord will "wipe away all tears" (Revelation 21:4 KJV). As Jesus entrusted them to the care of their living children, they too can trust Jesus to forever take care of the souls of the children they lost. One day, we will wake up in the eternal bode of Christ and find it filled with children who were denied a place in this life but who are the little ones of heaven.

Mental Health and Our Spiritual Crisis

I have been involved with the National Alliance on Mental Illness (NAMI) since 2010. I became involved with a local mental health group back in 2006 in Florida. What prompted my involvement? My own personal acquaintance with the issue. What I will say is that mental illnesses are real biological disorders of the mind. They are no one's fault, not the result of bad parenting or due to a bad environment, but neurobiological processes that have gone awry. A good film to see about schizophrenia is *A Beautiful Mind*, a movie about a real-life genius mathematician who slowly descended into his own personal nightmare, as he was caught up in hallucinations and delusions that seemed totally real but were not. His story is both gut-wrenching and inspiring.

Why connect the spiritual crisis with mental health then? Well, first, a mentally unhealthy society can aggravate the problems of people with biological issues. However, on a psychological level, it can also promote unhealthy patterns of behavior that hurt the mental health of people without biological issues.

I would argue that mental health and spiritual health are

inextricably linked. A recent study came out indicating that people who go to church are generally happier and mentally more stable than those who do not. Faith is good for people. Faith has been shown to improve mental and physical health, and it even improves longevity.[69]

Yet even institutions of faith can sometimes disappoint us. When my wife and I were living in the greater New York area, we went through a lot of stuff. The former president of our county chapter of NAMI had resigned, and as vice president, I became president at a time that my predecessor wanted to sue the board members. We were also members of a local church, and my wife was hospitalized because of excruciating abdominal pain, as a result of a fallopian tube torsion. Finally, after begging for help, our pastor came to visit and promised that meals were being prepared for us. No plans had been made, as we discovered later.

So for the first time, we sought counseling. The counselor assured us that we were fine; it was the area that was crazy. He then asked if he could bring God into the discussion. We said yes, of course it was. He then related the book of Romans to the issue of self-condemnation. This was the first time I had heard a trained counselor expound on Paul from a psychological standpoint. He said that many suffer from feelings of self-condemnation, and this is aggravated by circumstances that reinforce those existing insecurities. The counselor said that Christ, who delivers us from divine condemnation, also encourages us to forgive and accept ourselves as he does.

We were living in an area where the culture had mental health issues, with so many being angry, ill tempered, and dishonest as a way of life, and it was rubbing off on us; although, I think many of them suffered from self-condemnation, and were in need of spiritual and psychological healing. As I reflected on this experience, it became clear to me that cultures, as well as individuals, can become mentally and spiritually sick.

I met and befriended some wonderful people in our neighborhood, including the counselor who helped us. The local NAMI board awarded me with a plaque for excellent leadership and threw me a party. They were supportive of me. So I do not mean to make a blanket statement here. However, culture matters, and the values that shape it can bring out either the best in people or the worst.

A few years ago, there was a campaign in South Florida for employees of businesses and hotels to "be nice to the tourists." Apparently, Southern Floridians had developed the reputation of being unfriendly to tourists. Unfortunately, human nature is such that we become acclimated to the fish tank we live in and are often oblivious to the ways the tank could be improved. May we all pray to the Lord for a better insight about the fishbowls we find ourselves swimming in, lest we take on the worst characteristics of the other fish occupying our little world.

The Bible, as the counselor suggested, contains good advice for both spiritual and mental health. Interestingly, in recent years, good emotional and mental health has been linked to a sense of connection with others. The Old Testament speaks of individuals, but in their role as part of a people or giving birth to one. When we see ourselves in biblical terms, then we make the most vital connection with our creator and others.

Gratitude Is an Attitude

> Let your moderation be known unto all men. The Lord is at hand. Be careful, for nothing; but in everything by prayer and supplication with thanksgiving let your requests be made known to God. And the peace of God, which passeth all understanding, shall keep your minds and hearts through Christ Jesus. (Philippians 4:5–7 KJV)

One, Sunday, my wife and I were sitting through a sermon at the church in Florida where we first attended together, and the message was about giving thanks. There are rare occasions that I will listen to a sermon and not only process its message but act on it. The minister suggested to us that every time we see a veteran from one of the branches of the armed forces, we go up to that person and simply say, "Thank you for your service." I thought to myself, *That's easy enough to do.* After we moved from Florida to the New York area, I made it a point to do just that to every veteran I came across.

The first time I complimented a veteran, he jerked his head rather quickly and said, "Uh, what did you say to me?" I repeated my thanks for his service, and he responded rather curtly, "Th... th... thank you." He was obviously stunned that I offered thanks for his military service. I received similar reactions from other veterans to varying degrees, although they were all happy in the end that I expressed gratitude for their service.

I wondered why they were shocked. Then it occurred to me that we are living in times where gratitude is at a low point. We've become self-involved, with a great sense of entitlement. *I don't need to thank anyone,* we seem to think. *I deserve what I have or what I can get; society owes it me.* Messages in our popular culture, from institutions of learning, and even from our politicians reinforce the supposed nobility of the entitlement mentality. Why don't we call entitlement for what it is: ingratitude. Many well-off Americans are plagued with a deep and gnawing insecurity that they don't deserve what they possess; well, they don't.

I was fortunate enough to have been born into an affluent family; my father had been successful in the pharmaceutical industry and was later honored by his university for his contributions to the field of medicine. I enjoyed a childhood home with a swimming pool, in one of the poshest areas of South Florida.

I was along for the ride. It was entirely my father's accomplishment. Am I grateful for having enjoyed such a life? Yes. Did I deserve it? Honestly, who deserves to enjoy what others have earned? I was grateful, instead. I was thankful to have been born into such affluent circumstances.

It still bothers me when I hear of the grief that family members cause each other in fighting over the estate of their parents, as if their parents owed them anything. In the legal battles over estates, you can see the ugliness that entitlement and ingratitude bring out. As far as I'm concerned, my parents already gave me life and a wonderful start. Beyond that, they were under no other obligation, although my parents did give me more than that, for which I am grateful.

Aside from entitlement, we are also obsessed with the word *fairness*, as if that were a Christian cause. Shall we examine that claim? What is fair? Much of the obsession with the concept has to do with our sense of deprivation or loss. It is not fair that this person was promoted over me. It is not fair that others have more money that I do, or I was born into less than desirable circumstances.

In short, we use fairness as a club for the satisfaction of our own grievances for how life has treated us. I call it the philosophy of the sandbox. You know, the four-year-old kicking up a storm and screaming incessantly, "That's not fair!" At this point, I probably should add a disclaimer: I'm not saying there's anything wrong with wanting more justice in the world, but that is an unselfish pursuit. Most protestations about fairness concern ourselves.

Frankly, I do believe that life has been unfair to me, but for reasons quite different from how others might think: Life has been way too good to me. I have never known hunger or want. There was no draft to take me off to war. Why should I be satisfied when so many go hungry? Why should I be alive and free when so many of my generation have given their lives for my country, when so many around the world suffer under oppressive governments, when so many have died from disease or lack of food or clean water? Why should I be healthy when so many children are born with cancer, muscular dystrophy, or some other devastating condition?

In response to how well life has gone for us or the sacrifices of others, we can respond in one of four ways:

- We can try to convince ourselves that we deserve such blessings.
- We can feel a constant sense of guilt about it.
- We can numb ourselves to the reality.
- We can make the healthy choice of being grateful.

We can be grateful to God and others for what they have given to us and sacrificed for us. We can accept those gifts with thanksgiving.

Let us apply fairness to God, shall we? Was it fair that a perfect and blameless person offered his life for the sins of the world, or would it be fair that this man, who had done nothing wrong, be spared such agony, and the rest of us go to hell? The latter sounds quite fair to me. Why should a good guy do anything for a bunch of bad people? Fortunately, grace is not about what is fair or even right but about the lengths to which a loving Creator would go to sacrifice a part of himself for the objects of his affection. We should consider ourselves quite fortunate that God does not obsess over what is fair, like we do.

Finally, I have become convinced that happiness consists of receiving everything in life as a gift. Our parents gave us life. That was a gift. Someone offered us a job or a career. That was a gift. Others sacrificed their lives on our behalf in wars or conflict. That was a gift. Jesus offered himself on the cross for our behalf. That was the greatest gift. Receiving life with gratitude and thanksgiving is to be in touch with the real nature of our existence and to live life, acknowledging how we have been blessed and how we can be a blessing to others.

In the movie *Pay It Forward,* a young man gets the inspiration to pay a kindness forward rather than give back the blessings he received. He sparked a revolution where gratitude and giving became a way of life. Gratitude and thanksgiving lead to happiness. May it be so for us. Live with gratitude.

What Was the Significance of Saul Changing His Name to Paul?

Saul of Tarsus was travelling down to Damascus, Syria, for the purpose of persecuting more Christians when he had a blazing experience of light and met Jesus. As one chosen by Christ to reach the world, he chose the name of Paul. Paul was in fact his Roman name.

Many scholars see no deeper significance than that he simply used his Roman name because he was travelling in the Roman world, and it is unbiblical, in their opinion, to read any deeper significance into it. That's a valid theory but one that troubles me as a Christian pilgrim because there is a deeply biblical reason to support such a contention that many scholars dismiss, but there is ample reason to believe it. Frankly, I find the dismissal of the idea to be glib and shallow.[70] Paul made a very personal connection with Abraham, as I see it. John Chrysostom, an ancient church father, even made the point that Paul took on a "new Gentile name instead of his Jewish name, as an indication of his new office, the Apostle of the Gentiles, … but this is only conjecture, on which I insist not."[71]

Abraham began his life as Abram, which is Hebrew for "high father." In Genesis 17:5, he changed his name, by the command of God, to Abraham, which in Hebrew means "father of a multitude." We see the significance of Abraham to Paul's own theology in Romans:

> Therefore, the promise comes by faith, so that it may be by grace and be guaranteed to all Abraham's offspring—not only to those who are of the law but also to those who have the faith of Abraham. He is the father of us all. (Romans 4:16 NIV)

We see this significance in Abraham's own story.

> Abram believed the Lord, and he credited it to him as righteousness. (Genesis 15:6 NIV)

Paul (originally Saul) was a student of Gamaliel, the grandson of Hillel and thus an heir of his liberal Pharisaic tradition. Gamaliel, in fact, did much to secure Hillel's legacy in Judaism.[72] Saul's whole life was centered around the study of the law and becoming a faithful Pharisee and defender of Torah law as the foundation of a righteous life. His anger toward the Christians or the members of the Way centered around their disregard for the law and for following the false messiah Jesus.

Ultimately, Saul is confronted by Jesus himself and finds himself on a distinctly different path. He begins to rework the foundations of Judaic theology based on his new faith in Jesus. Yet Saul does not begin with a discussion of Moses or the Torah, as one would expect from a trained rabbinic scholar, but with Abraham, who was personally called by God to be the father of a people.

> The Lord said to Abram, "Leave your country, your people and your father's household and go to the land I will show you. I will make you into a great nation and I will bless you; I will make your name great, and you will be my blessing. I will bless those who bless you and whoever curses you I will curse; and all peoples on earth will be blessed through you." (Genesis 12:1–3 NIV)

Compare this encounter with Yahweh to the encounter Saul has with Jesus on the road to Damascus.

> As he journeyed, he came near Damascus and suddenly a light shone around him from heaven. The he fell to the ground, and heard a voice saying to him, "Saul, Saul, why are you persecuting me?" And he said, "Who are you Lord?" Then the Lord said, "I am Jesus whom you are persecuting. It is hard for you to kick against the goads." (Acts 9:1–5 NIV)

Later, the Lord Jesus instructs a Christian named Ananias to receive Saul. Ananias objects by pointing out Saul's role in persecuting those who professed the name of Jesus, and Ananias's objection is answered as follows: "But the Lord said to him, 'Go, for he is a chosen vessel of Mine to bear My name before Gentiles, kings, and the children of Israel. For I will show him how many things he must suffer for My name's sake'" (Acts 9:15–16 NIV).

Saul went from being a person who was devoted to the law to a person like Abraham; he found a righteousness through Christ apart from the law. As a conservative rabbi in my ministerial association once shared with me, "We are okay with Jesus; it is Paul we have a problem with." A reasonable criticism, since it was Paul who actively worked to sever the church from its moorings to Jewish law and thus bring about a new universal religion based on the righteousness that comes by faith and trust alone.

A person who found righteousness through faith and obedience alone. Like Abram, Saul had been personally chosen by God to create many descendants of faith, including Jews and Gentiles alike. Like Abram, Saul would change his name to reflect his chosen role, a reflection of Paul being inspired by Abraham's example, and God's command to him to make that change.

If Christ is the second Adam, could it also stand to reason that Paul was the second Abraham? I think so. The critics of my position are quick to point out that Saul was not commanded by God to change his Jewish name to his Roman one, the way Abram was so commanded to change his name. I agree. Changing his name was Paul's own choice, but it reflected his desire to identify with Abraham.

He went from his Jewish name of Saul to his Roman name of Paul to reflect the change in his being and his chosen status as an apostle to the world. His change from being a person whose life and faith was centered on the Jewish law to a person whose life was centered on the kind of faith that Abraham exercised, before there even was a law. In a significant sense, Paul was the heir of Abraham's mantle and was chosen by God to assume it; at least that's how he understood it. We modern people tend to forget that human beings for most of our history have not been creatures of reason but mythology. We read of Paul's calling in Galatians:

I want you to know, brothers and sisters, that the gospel I preached is not of human origin. I did not receive from any man, nor was I taught it; rather I received it by a revelation from Jesus Christ.

For you have heard of my previous way of life in Judaism, how intensely I persecuted the church of God and tried to destroy it. I was advancing in Judaism beyond many of my own age among my people and was extremely zealous for the traditions of my fathers. But when God, who set me apart from my mother's womb and called me by his grace, was pleased to reveal his Son in me so that I might preach him among the Gentiles, my immediate response was not to consult any human being. I did not go up to Jerusalem to see those who were apostles before I was, but I went to Arabia. Later I returned to Damascus. (Galatians 1:11–17 NIV)

Paul, no doubt, wondered where his life lay in God's salvific scheme. Paul was like Abraham in the sense that John the Baptist was the Elijah to come, as Jesus described him. John the Baptist was not literally the return of Elijah, but metaphorically speaking, he was the one who assumed Elijah's prophetic mantle. Paul similarly assumed the spiritual mantle of Abraham.[73]

Which raises a question: Am I just splitting hairs here? Perhaps, but it has troubled me that many scholars seem to dismiss the obvious point, of the way in which Paul saw himself and his significance, and how he was chosen to bring to the world that righteousness of faith. Abraham received this blessing of God without the necessity of the law, and that faith was within reach of every person through the finished work of Christ, according to Paul. We read in Galatians, "Understand, then, that those who have faith are children of Abraham. Scripture foresaw that God would justify the Gentiles by faith and announced the gospel in advance to Abraham: 'All nations will be blessed through you.' So those who rely on faith are blessed along with Abraham, the man of faith ... Clearly, no one who relies on the law is justified before God, because the 'righteous will live by faith'" (Galatians 3:7–9, 11 NIV).

After my wife read this section of my book, she asked me, "How would this matter to the reader?" I recognized immediately that this was a good question. Saul, by changing from his Jewish name to his Roman one, was modelling for us symbolically that in Christ, we become something new. We become a new creature or creation. We are now serving a different master and purpose. Paul expressed it succinctly this way: "This means that anyone who belongs to Christ has become a new person. The old life has is gone; a new life has begun" (2 Corinthians 5:17 NLT).

Materialism Destroys Spiritual Happiness

> Whoever finds their life will lose it, and whoever loses their life for my sake will find it. (Matthew 10:39 NIV)

Our materialism has become a form of neurosis. I love things for what they can deliver and not for what slick advertising promises. I remember as a small child our family made frequent trips through the Smoky Mountains, to the fun village of Gatlinburg, Tennessee. I am old enough to remember our old car that only had a fan and no air conditioning. During the hot summer, the fan felt like air from Hades.

What a difference Dad's new Oldsmobile made with the newfangled air conditioning installed in it. It was like a cold wind from heaven in the relentless heat and humidity that accompanied our regular trips to Gatlinburg. Seeing TV shows in color when Dad bought our first color set in 1970 was a site to behold. This happened after our old black-and-white set overloaded and shorted out from a lightning storm. Yet I could enjoy these simple pleasures because I was content with being in a family where I was loved and secure.

The sad truth about materialism is that it robs us of our ability to enjoy material things for what they offer us. People with a materialist mindset expect things to provide them not only material comforts and enjoyment but a sense of status, purpose, and meaning.

Therefore, materialistic people feel compelled to wear certain brands of suits, drive certain kinds of cars, or have a television the size of their wall. It is about things as symbols of power, status, and importance. For the materialist, it is not simply about the utility of things, or even their enjoyment, but the importance and power they presumably confer upon their owners, in their own eyes and in the eyes of their peers, the culture, and society.

Whereas Dad, who was content to buy Sears suits for his corporate job simply for the utility of looking professional, was surrounded by others who wore pricier luxury suits because it made them feel important. My dad never needed a status symbol to make him feel worthwhile. He found value in himself. Taking after his example, I have endeavored to find value in myself as well.

Frankly, it is not possible for things to offer us meaning and purpose, although the illusion that it can provide us these things fuels manic consumer consumption and exorbitant debt. Our whole advertising culture cultivates this illusion in every way possible. Yet it is an illusion and a destructive one. Jesus said, "Beware! Guard against every kind of greed. Life is not measured by how much you own" (Luke 12:15 NLT).

The sad reality for many in America is that they do not own things, as much as things own them. Our pocketbooks, our credit cards, and even our souls are prisoners to accumulation, liability, clutter, and debt. The explosion in the storage facility business in America is a sign, I believe, of the accumulation neurosis.

Many Americans are typically accumulating more stuff then they can possibly store in their own homes. Hence, the need for more and more storage facility containers, barns, and silos, and this storage cost eats up a large portion of their income, just to provide a space for their stuff.

It has been noted that there is an epidemic of depression and melancholy in our nation. How can we account for this unsettling development in the most prosperous capitalist country in the world. Japan, another affluent capitalist country, similarly has a record suicide rate. In fact, more Japanese children committed suicide between 2016 and 2017 than any year since 1986; it was the highest suicide rate in thirty years.[74] Our Lord says that our "life is not measured by how much you own" (Luke 12:15 NLT). Yet things are what people in developed countries pursue as an obsession.

I read recently that according to a survey, 70 percent of the millennial generation believe in socialism. Kind of ironic, when one considers the computer tablets, i-Phones, and fashion that many of them wear. One could argue that they are merely spoiled and fail to see the benefits of capitalism, although many of them are struggling with student debt and jobs with meager pay, and this could in part account for the appeal.[75]

Yet I am persuaded that this is a symptom of a deeper syndrome. Unbeknownst to these millennials, what I really believe is that they are disillusioned with materialism. Like their boomer parents, they bought into the illusion of material happiness and are deeply unsettled by how little authentic meaning it has offered them. What makes matters worse is that they have grown up in a time of unprecedented business and political corruption; they watched, as boomers were willing to do anything to empower themselves at the expense of others.

Some think that the sharing supposedly involved in socialism is the answer or acts of service or becoming involved in ecology. There is nothing wrong about wanting to share or caring more about the world. Yet I have noticed that despite such idealism, many of them still seem empty and come across as a little self-righteous, blaming the previous generation for all the problems in the world.

The millennial generation has yet to realize that you go back just a generation or two, you find people in our society who were happier and more content with less. Much less. Again, if I were to criticize the emerging generation, I would say that there is too little curiosity about the lives of previous generations and too much judgment about them.

I think what these millennials long for is a society with a soul. What they are really craving is for their own souls to be nourished; our materialist society cannot provide that nourishment. Contrary to what they may believe, socialists can also be materialists, believing that if only everyone gets a larger share of the material wealth, then this will bring everyone happiness, when in fact, this belief only plays into the same illusion.

Comparing the writings of Karl Marx and Charles Dickens is a revealing study of how two perceptive people could look at the same society and the same issues and come to vastly different conclusions.

Karl Marx was a social critic and political theorist. Charles Dickens was a social critic and novelist. Both lived during the tumultuous time of Europe's emerging Industrial Revolution. Both wrote about the misery of the working classes and the indifference of the capitalists. Marx wrote political treatises about the nature of the misery and offered solutions. Dickens wrote novels about the nature of the misery and offered solutions. Both saw important significance in the French Revolution.

Yet both came to completely different perspectives about the nature of the real problem. For Marx, materialism was everything. He called his perspective dialectical materialism. All of history was about the struggles between emerging social classes. The last epoch had been about the nobility and the capitalists. The current and in Marx's opinion final epoch, it had become about the capitalists he called the bourgeoisie and the working classes he called the proletariat.[76]

For Dickens, the soul was everything. His perspective was that of Christianity. He acknowledged that there was a struggle between classes, but the real problem was not in the social arrangements per se, but in the character of those who exercised power. The French Revolution was the subject of his novel *A Tale of Two Cities* and argued that the vices present in the nobility were equally present in the Revolutionary government.

The noblest moment in the novel is the sacrificial action of an individual who showed himself to be better than the typical member of either party. This man submits himself to the guillotine, willingly, to save someone else, as it is eloquently expressed in the novel:

> It is a far, far better thing that I do, than I have ever done; it is a far, far better rest that I go to than I have ever known.[77]

Whereas Dickens saw faith as a critical answer to material and political despair, Marx saw religion as an "opiate" or a drug that dulled the senses of people about the real nature of their situation and pacified them from doing anything about it. Dickens instead saw that a recognition of the soul could help individuals see, with clarity, how others were being unfairly used and exploited, as eternal creatures who needed to be cherished and cared for.

This idea is present generally in his novels but is brought to its ultimate clarity in *A Christmas Carol*. Ebenezer Scrooge is initially portrayed as the archetype cold and calculating capitalist who saw people, as well as things, as commodities that were either useful or of no value. Interestingly enough, as we explore Scrooge's past in the novel, it becomes apparent that he was not always this way, but a man who was so deeply wounded by life that he eventually ceases to value his own soul, in his belief that only material accumulation mattered or could bring him solace.

By the end of the novel, which concludes on Christmas Day, Scrooge comes to the startling revelation that greed and materialism had become his prison and not his real comfort, and they had prevented him from properly grieving, living, or loving.

It was not that his wealth alone had made him a miserable person, but his belief that it was the only thing worth living for had.

I would like to note that a boisterous celebration of Christmas had gone out of vogue in England by the time of Dickens's writing. *A Christmas Carol* did much to bring the celebration of Christmas back in England. Many criticize Christmas for its materialism. However, that fact alone has never bothered me. It is my contention that Christmas is the one time of the year where even materialism and capitalism are obliged to acknowledge the Lordship of Christ.

Thus, while changing social arrangements was the key to understanding Marx, the key to understanding Dickens is that all arrangements can be corrupted by the inhuman materialism of people, and until that changes, nothing has changed in the souls of people. It is our perspectives that need a revolution and not necessarily our social and economic arrangements, per se.

As a Christian pilgrim, I am troubled that our material culture has become spiritually toxic. Many in the emerging generations know the "price of everything and the value of nothing." The rediscovery of the value of living, and how material things should complement the meaning of our life rather than define it, could be a liberating revelation for many. My prayers will continue to be directed toward that end.

The New Atheism and a Convincing Apologetic

New atheism is influencing many millennials who are being exposed to a negative view of God, promoted by the likes of the late Christopher Hitchens, Richard Dawkins, and college professors who were looking to undo their faith in God. This atheism is promoted with a religious zeal that parallels that of traditional religion.

I have noticed there is a strong appeal among college students for this liberation from the primitive superstition of belief. The assumptions of atheism are even seeping into the Christian faith. A survey in 2001 revealed that more than half of American Catholics, Lutherans, Methodists, and Presbyterians "believed that Jesus had sinned."[78]

This current situation reminds me of when I was a student at a community college in the early 1980s. I took a humanities course with a self-avowed atheist professor. He challenged the class to write a paper defending the existence of God. Well, I never could pass up on a challenge. The professor was a determinist, as well as an atheist, and he stated that God could create creatures who always did right if he so chose, but not ones who could choose either good or evil. Free will, in his opinion, was an illusion.

I also remember this professor ridiculing the idea that God could make contradictory ideas possible. "Could God make a square circle?" he retorted. This assertion seemed impossible to refute at the time; I had no answer for it, and neither did my classmates. I wish I knew what I know now. The existence of two seemingly contradictory ideas, that are at the same time held to be true, is called a paradox. I did not know about paradoxes as a college sophomore, but I have come to realize that many of the greatest truths are paradoxes. That God could be three persons and yet one divine being is just such a paradox, in this case $1 + 2 = 1$ or $3 = 1$.

Let us take modern physics, for instance. Boy, I wish I also knew about this as a college sophomore. According to modern physics, the way matter, energy, and space behave in Einstein's macro universe and the way they behave in the micro or quantum universe of Max Plank are completely different.

No one has successfully come up with a testable hypothesis that would explain this apparent paradox. So-called string theory has been proffered as a solution, but it apparently is untestable. In short, the contradictory forces of our universe constitute what some could describe as an ongoing "square circle." These contradictory forces make up two sides of a paradox that is more profound than either alone. Yet if there is a God, this complexity is surely a reflection of his eternal mind.

Free will versus determinism is a popular theme in philosophical writings. I then researched a paper defending the existence of God, free will, and evil based on a principle in physics known as Heisenberg's principle of uncertainty. According to this principle, the cause and outcomes of actions on a quantum or particle level are not predetermined, nor can they be predicted with certainty.[79] So, as my argument goes, if the universe is free, then it stands to reason that so are we. I received an A in this class, and yes, I am bragging.

There will be times in your life of faith when others will challenge the credibility and intelligence of your faith. Some of those challenges are going to appear intimidating, because those who have no belief in God often give more thought to these issues than those who do. Don't be discouraged by that fact; as a troubled Christian pilgrim, I have been in that spot more than once. The answer to such a challenge is for people of faith to think deeply about the intellectual as well the emotional reasons for believing in God. We are to offer a defense or apologia as we read in 1 Peter, "But in your hearts regard Christ the Lord as holy, ready at any time to give a defense to anyone who asks you for a reason for the hope that is in you" (1 Peter 3:15 CSB).

Theologians call the practice of mounting such a defense apologetics. There have been many theologians and lay Christians who have sought to provide reasoned arguments for the Christian faith. I have always been impressed by natural theologian William Paley, although he is unfairly dismissed by many, and yet the strength of his arguments continue to challenge many. He is known for the argument from design, the teleological argument for the existence of God. I happen to think it is a strong argument for God's existence, but it is deeply misunderstood, in my estimation.

The key in examining Paley's main argument is the idea that the existence of a watch implies the existence of watchmaker. Paley suggests this as a "proof" or an "inference" one could make based on the available data, but not a definitive conclusion. I think this is an especially important distinction. Natural theologians were not trying to prove the existence of God from nature but to show from nature why a belief in God as disclosed in revelatory religion was not unreasonable. Faith was still required, but a reasonable step of faith, that is consistent with logic.[80]

In other words, suppose some member of an isolated and remote tribe were to discover a Timex watch. They could not read or discern what the Timex label meant, but they could see that it was a ticking organism of some kind with hands that moved over its face. Likely, the tribesmen would reasonably infer that it was the product of a god or some strange tribe but not something that simply happened. In other words, they would make a reasonable inference or deduction that it was product of intelligence.

Natural theologians, therefore, were not full of the hubris to believe that they could prove from nature that God existed, but to show from nature that the complexity of its structures and organisms implied or strongly suggested an intelligent design. This alone does not prove the existence of God, but in the opinion of William Paley, it showed that while a belief in God may stand above reason, it certainly does not contradict it.

Have you ever watched the History Channel? There is a show on ancient aliens who supposedly helped us build our civilization and sped up our evolution. It is based on the ideas of Erich Von Daniken, who wrote a book called *Chariots of the Gods* and proposed this hypothesis based on his interpretation of ancient historical artifacts and records. He even includes the Bible in his hypothesis of extraterrestrial influence on our human development. I remember first reading his book back in the 1970s, when as a youngster I had strong interest in UFOs and the whole ET subject. I am not so enamored today.[81]

However, many scientists, including the late astrophysicist Sir Fredrich Hoyle, wrote eloquently about the mathematical improbabilities of organic evolution as it has been promulgated by anthropologists. Since the time of Hoyle, many other scientists are finding the idea of random chance and natural forces as the reason for our existence more and more scientifically problematic.

Hoyle asserted "that the probability of life originating at random is so utterly minuscule as to make the random concept absurd." He further articulated that our intelligence must be the product of an even greater intelligence and asserted that his conclusions about the improbability of life were "big enough to bury Darwin." He even presented the idea of extraterrestrial beings seeding our world as a credible explanation for things, as was the possibility of organic chemicals riding to Earth on a meteor.[82] Hoyle, a religious skeptic, nevertheless asserted that:

> It is no more likely that our world has evolved out of chaos than that a hurricane, blowing through a junkyard, should create a Boeing 747.[83]

I agree with Von Daniken and Hoyle, at least partially. Their theories do not answer the question of how the extraterrestrials came into existence or how life got started. Nevertheless, I do believe that an extraterrestrial was the creator of organic life and the world. I just happen to give that ET the name of God.

Many astronomers are also reconsidering our place in the universe. Physicist Enrico Fermi presented a famous paradox in 1952: "If the universe is teeming with life, then where is it?"[84] Astronomers are coming to understand that earth is indeed a special place and that the conditions that gave rise to life are exceedingly rare. Scientists have discovered that the universe is very hostile to the development of life.

Why is it that Jupiter catches most of the objects that would otherwise hurtle toward the earth? How is it that we have a moon that does such an excellent job of regulating the tides in our oceans? How did the earth find itself in the perfect orbit around the sun for the climate conditions from which carbon life could flourish? Why is it that we are perfectly positioned in our galaxy to observe the stars in it? These facts raise this question: Doesn't this suggest an intelligence at work?

So why all the zealotry of those in the evolution field? Isn't science supposed to be about gaining a sound understanding of our physical world based on observation, evidence, experimentation, discovery, and hypothesis? It should be, but as my scientist wife has pointed out to me, scientists are also people of prejudice, like the rest of us. They have ideas that they can tenaciously hold onto, even in the face of contradictory evidence.

As a Christian, my faith does not hinge on evolution or special creation but the fact that God made the world. Geneticist Francis Collins, former director of the Human Genome Project, is a theistic evolutionist who came to believe in a creator based on his study of DNA, which he described in a book I encourage everyone to read called *The Language of God*.[85] Recently, there have been design advocates who claim that organic life is made up of irreducible machines at the cellular level, without which life itself cannot exist. You can be sure that these intelligent design advocates have caused a firestorm in the scientific community.[86]

Who is right? I am not sure, but as a troubled Christian pilgrim, it bothers me that so many in the scientific community are determined to censor intelligent design and even theistic evolution advocates, because of what I believe is a philosophical and anti-religious bias. Let us suppose that as an atheist, I hinge the validity of my worldview on random natural forces as the explanation for everything. Then, naturally, I am going to defend the theory of evolution, or at least a nontheistic interpretation of it, with zeal. This is not because of the integrity of science but because of a worldview that I hold.

Truthfully, it is beyond the capacity of science to prove or disprove the existence of a being who underlies all of reality. Where do you begin to test or evaluate that proposition? All science can do in this regard is draw intuitive or rational inferences from the evidence, just like William Paley, Francis Collins, and intelligent design advocates have. Paul expressed that such an inference could be made:

> For since the creation of the world God's invisible qualities—his eternal power and

divine nature—having been clearly seen, being understood from what is made, so that people are without excuse. (Romans 1:20 NIV)

Just because the inference that such believing people draw contradicts an atheistic inference does not make them wrong in their science, as I see it. It just makes them people who have come to a different philosophical conclusion concerning what they have observed.

When Contrived Theological Language Destroys New Testament Theology

The current obsession in mainline churches with changing the language of the Trinity is a troubling development. It is one thing for theology to accommodate itself to the human situation. It is quite another thing to be completely rewritten by it. There appears to be a movement in the mainline churches to feminize or eliminate any gender references to the Trinity. This way, they have rescinded the traditional triune formula of God the Father, Son, and Holy Spirit. Why? Part of it, I believe, is the impact of feminism on Christian theology using contrived language. *Contrived* is defined as something that is made or arranged artificially, rather than something that naturally arises from common knowledge or sources.

There is an outright revolt against any masculine references to God. Somehow referring to God as the Heavenly Father is seen as paying homage to patriarchy and male oppression. Bad experiences with fathers, and what is called toxic masculinity, which refers to the obnoxious aspects of maleness, are also offered as reasons to alter the language in a contrived way, and make it either feminine or gender neutral. My response to such concerns is to point out that Jesus Christ made it clear that his Father was better than any earthly parent. We read in Luke:

> You fathers—if your child asks for a fish, do you give them a snake instead? Or if they ask for an egg, do you give them a scorpion? Of course not! So, if you sinful people know how to give good gifts to your children, how much more will your heavenly father give the Holy Spirit to those who ask him? (Luke 11:11–13 NLT)

I like the way the English Standard Version describes fathers: "If you then, who are evil" (Luke 11:13 ESV). What are we to surmise from this? God is better than any father, all of whom are sinful and even evil by comparison. Women are not necessarily depicted in scripture as the best of human beings, either. I offer Jezebel and Herodias, the wife of King Herod Antipas, as examples. Consider, for a moment, the children who have been abused by their mothers or husbands who have been mistreated by their wives. Does that mean, therefore, that one should find something distasteful about feminine references to God?

This gets to the crux of my pet peeve here. Should we examine our gender, psychological, and sociological hang-ups in the light of scripture, or rewrite scripture and theology to suit those hang-ups? There is room for discussion, but at what point will anyone be satisfied with the rewrites, or will theology continue to drift along to suit the agendas of malcontents, rather than reflect what we find in scripture?

There is a contemporary mainline hymnal that has in it selections of classical and beloved hymns, rewritten with contrived theological language, for the purpose of suiting the agendas of malcontents. It troubles me that traditional songs, which are otherwise a joy to sing, have been rendered musically awkward, spiritually sterile, and practically unsingable.

I probably sound harsh at this point, but the church retained its theological language for centuries because it sought to be faithful to the Bible. It did not retain its language for the overt or covert purpose of oppressing any gender or class of people, as I see it.

Frankly, Heavenly Father is a relational reference, first and foremost. I think many attribute the idea of a heavenly father with the anthropomorphic notion that God has a set of male genitals. Anthropomorphism is to attribute to God certain human qualities. This is a crude misunderstanding of a broader concept, and yes, it is meaningful that God became incarnate in a man, a vastly different kind of man. Besides, there are plenty of nongender references like rock, angel of the Lord, or shepherd to demonstrate the variety of images of God in the Old and New Testaments.[87]

Yes, Jesus was a human being and man, but unlike any other. He was not one who confirmed all the worst images of patriarchy; instead, his life and teachings were a living refutation of it. No single person in history did more than Jesus to elevate the stature and esteem of women. Some have even called Jesus the first feminist. He showed mercy for their failings, exalted their sensitivity, recruited them for his mission, and made a woman the first witness to his resurrection.

No one elevated children or their value in the world more than Jesus did. Let us consider that if God is a better kind of parent and father, then Jesus is a superior kind of man and human being, thus transforming the whole purpose, meaning, and mission of gender as we commonly think of it. Jesus put forward a feminine image of God in his lament about Jerusalem:

> Jerusalem, Jerusalem, who kills the prophets and stones those who are sent to her. How often I wanted to gather your children together, as a hen gathers her chicks under her wings, but you were not willing. (Luke 13:34 CSB)

Jesus put forth a different conception of manhood. There is the old trite saying that "Big boys don't cry." Yet Jesus cried often and for many reasons. As a man, he expressed the full range of emotions, even those that some see as inappropriate for men. In the shortest verse in the New Testament, we read in John 11:35

(as found in most versions), "Jesus wept." This was in response to Mary, the sister of Lazarus, who was distraught that he had come too late to prevent her brother from dying.

Our Lord was a man who could be moved by the emotions of others and had a keen heart. If only those who are fixated on changing our New Testament language studied more deeply the sensitivity to be found in the New Testament itself, this would change their whole perspective.

Yet as a Christian pilgrim, I am troubled that people pushing an inclusive-language agenda are not interested in exploring the full range of New Testament images of God. Instead, they use contrived theological language to deconstruct New Testament faith altogether.

What Is the Real Cure for Racism?

The identity politics we are plagued with today is at odds, I believe, with the ethic of Dr. Martin Luther King, who preached reconciliation among various peoples. What is inclusive about an ideology that pits one group of people against another? This is a very divisive development, as I see it. This is less about evaluating people by the content of their character and more about judging them according to their race or social standing. As I recall, there was a politician who used the term "deplorables" to describe a whole swathe of our fellow citizens.

This troubles me as a Christian pilgrim, in terms of how our racial discussion has experienced such terrible setbacks in recent years from this kind of politics. Politicians who used to preach the virtue of racial reconciliation and brotherhood now find it more politically profitable to incite racial and class animosities.

This has had a chain reaction, whereby identity groups of all kinds have found it easier to enlist recruits for their divisive causes. As an example, you have the emergence of safe spaces, dorms, and even graduations ceremonies that are race exclusive.

School administrators and professors have been threatened, or even fired, if they did not agree with such agendas. The Civil Rights movement used to be about ending hateful tribalism, but now it appears that hateful tribalism has become cool and chic in politics and academia. This trend has also fostered some unsettling repercussions across the race and political spectrum.[88]

There was quite a controversy over the activism group called Black Lives Matter. I always thought that the title was unfortunate, even though I'm sure I understand what its real intention was. BLM was intended to communicate the desperate message that many in the black community feel that their lives are threatened and their concerns have been ignored. However, I think the moniker of Black Lives Also Matter would have done a better job of conveying their intended message.

Do I think racial prejudice is a big problem in America? Actually, no. All studies on the matter indicate that such prejudice is on the decline. However, I think there is a more pressing problem in America. Some have asserted that there is something called white privilege. Yes, I think there is such a thing, although not because white people do not share in the same social or economic problems as people of color. There are plenty of poor, drug-addicted, and imprisoned white people.

So what is white privilege, then? It revolves around what those like me, white Caucasians, have not been subjected to. Police do not stop us in strange neighborhoods because of our race; we are generally not discriminated against on that basis in employment, school admission, lodging, or restaurants and theaters; and we are not persecuted for being white. This has been the African American experience, although Irish, Hispanic, and Jewish people, who are also generally white, have experienced the same treatment. Germans and Italians were also subject to discrimination during the two world wars, and the internment of the Japanese during World War II is a matter of historical record. Asians in general have also experienced some of this kind of treatment.

I first learned fully about the black experience in elementary school when I read a book that offered a summary of black history called *The Black American*. The experiences of people of color from slavery through persecution has shaped the psyches of people of color in a very traumatic way. For them, the trauma remains, even though the rest of us would rather blissfully go on and forget that such evils happened in America.

Also, having lived and worked in South Florida, I discovered that Jamaicans and other Caribbean people of color look at the issue of race differently than either white Americans or African Americans. They are apt to see all people as good, unless you give them reasons to believe otherwise. I found my experience with island people to be like a fresh wind from heaven, which means that the filter through which we as Americans look at the issue of race is not universal but particular to our own experience, and by God's grace, we can learn from others who come out of a different experience.

We are wired to the experience of our racial identity. We look at the world through five filters. The first filter is of our immediate family, relatives, and family history. The second filter is that of our broader race and ethnic heritage. The third filter is what we were taught, growing up, about people of other racial, ethnic, national, and religious identities. The fourth filter is our personal experience with people from other groups. The fifth filter is how we make sense of and integrate the other four filters into our view of ourselves and others.

So again, what is the pressing problem? The real overarching problem in America, as I perceive it, is not racial hatred but racial indifference. If something does not affect me or my group, then why should I care about it? This situation reminds me of a passage out of Revelations:

> So, because you are lukewarm, and neither hot, nor cold, I am going to vomit you out of my mouth. (Revelation 3:16 HCSB)

You might be surprised if I told you that the opposite of love is not hate but indifference; in other words, to feel nothing for others or their plight. This does not just apply to the issue of race but to a host of social problems that people are ready to ignore, because they just don't care. As someone involved in the issue of homelessness, mental health, and the foster care system, I see what indifference has produced, in terms of the pervasive and unaddressed problems that have persisted in these areas.

That is unfortunate, because our society, like all others, is a quilt, sown together from many different fabrics. When one fabric begins to strain and break, it begins to affect everything else sown into the quilt. Those who are indifferent watch idly by as the threads in that fabric begin to break, in the belief that none of this is going to affect them, only to make the sad discovery that indifference eventually catches up with us all and affects us in the form of economic costs, protests, crime, violence, and social disruption.

So where do go from here? What diminishes prejudice about other groups? Oddly enough, it usually involves getting to know people as individuals. I have discovered that you start with what you admire and like about a particular individual, and you look backward to the possible influences that their upbringing and racial, ethnic, and other influences may have had on them, to make them a person you like. Conversely, we sometimes severely judge an entire group because of a bad experience with a member of that group. Group identity is, in fact, meaningless without an understanding of the individuals who make it up. Yet the presence of sin is prevalent in the whole human family, as Paul writes:

> None is righteous, no, not one; no one understands; no one seeks for God. All have turned aside; together they have become worthless; no one does good, not even one. (Romans 3:10–12 ESV)

Let us look at the human family, shall we? Let us consider some prominent individuals who have comprised many of these groups. As someone of German ancestry, it bothers me that out of my kindred came evil individuals like Nazi dictator Adolf Hitler, his propaganda minister Joseph Goebbels, or his SS henchman and concentration camp butcher, Heinrich Himmler.

Yet was not Dwight Eisenhower, Supreme Allied commander during World War II and US president in the 1950s, also of German ancestry? German industrialist Oskar Schindler used his influence to save Jews by employing them in his factories during World War II. Konrad Adenauer, the principle founder of the German Federal Republic after World War II, was even praised by Winston Churchill as one of the greatest democratic leaders of all time.

How about theologian Dietrich Bonhoeffer, who was part of an organized effort to resist Hitler, and whose life was ended by a Nazi SS officer? I could consider the legacy of my own German great-great-grandfathers, who fought in the American Civil War for the Union. Werner von Braun started out engineering rockets for the Nazis but was later responsible for developing the rockets of the US space program.

The Jewish people have been gifted with great people across the arts and sciences. Leaders such as British Prime Minister Benjamin Disraeli and US Senator Jacob Javits were Jewish. Theoretical physicist Albert Einstein was Jewish, and so was Robert Oppenheimer, the father of the atomic bomb. However, Meyer Lansky, one of the godfathers of organized crime in America, was also Jewish, as well as gangster Bugsy Siegel, the founder of Las Vegas. Caiaphas, the chief religious leader of the Sanhedrin who persecuted Jesus, was Jewish, but then so were Jesus and his apostles, along with two other religious leaders of the Sanhedrin, Joseph of Arimathea and Nicodemus, who supported Jesus.

Infamous organized crime bosses Alfonse Capone and John Gotti were Italian, as were other crime families in America. However, electrical engineer Guglielmo Marconi, who invented the radio, was Italian, and so was Enrico Fermi, the father of nuclear energy. Infamous fascist dictator Benito Mussolini was Italian, but two of the greatest mayors in the history of New York City, Fiorello

LaGuardia and Rudolph Giuliani, were also Italian, and so was Supreme Court Justice Anton Scalia. Roman soldiers tortured and crucified Jesus, but a Roman captain was praised by Jesus for his faith, and one proclaimed his divinity at the Crucifixion, according to Gospel accounts.

There are those of African heritage, like Dr. Charles Drew, who invented lifesaving blood plasma, and George Washington Carver, who did groundbreaking work with the peanut. African Americans Katherine Johnson, Dorothy Vaughn, and Mary Jackson were featured in the movie *Hidden Figures*; they possessed engineering, computer, and math skills that were critical to the success of the US space program. African American Benjamin Banneker, scientist and surveyor, helped to map out and design the city of Washington DC. Crispus Attucks, a former slave, was the first person to die in the American Revolution. Ruthless dictator Idi Amin was African, but so were Bishop Desmond Tutu and Nelson Mandela.[89]

Serbia is a nation rife with ethnic and racial strife, and an assassin from that country sparked World War I. Serbian leader Slobodan Milosevic attempted genocide against a whole group of people in his country. Yet from that country also came electrical engineer Nicola Tesla, who revolutionized electric power distribution around the world through his invention of alternating current.

The biggest mass murderer in history was Red Chinese leader Mao Zedong. Yet Christian Chinese leader Chiang Kai-shek would leave mainland China to become the founder of the Republic of Taiwan, a thriving and free society. Joseph Stalin, a Russian ruler, was the second biggest mass murder in history. Yet Russian authors Leo Tolstoy and Alexander Solzhenitsyn are also among the greatest Christian writers

I could go on and name numerous examples from other groups. However, I guess my point is this: When you analyze it objectively, the potential for good and evil, genius and idiocy, or bigotry and tolerance is evenly distributed throughout the human family.

> Choose this day whom you will serve ... But as for
> me and my house, we will serve the Lord. (Joshua
> 24:15 ESV)

My mother wrote a song many years ago that reflects the wonder and beauty of God's creation of humanity:

> God made color to brighten the world. He made ...
> their hair, skin and eyes as multicolored as the
> skies.

Regardless of our race and influences, we are all free to choose what kind of person we will be and who and what we will serve. I am troubled as a Christian pilgrim that many have slipped into believing that our individual life choices, regarding our actions and attitudes, are of no consequence in determining who we become, when in reality, those choices shape our character and destiny.

Sex and the Idols of Our Time

I have known gay people most of my life. Growing up in South Florida, I lived near one of the largest gay communities in America. I was there in 1977 for the famous gay rights ordinance referendum that stirred enormous controversy in Dade County; I was in junior high school at the time. Anita Bryant, a local celebrity, Miss America winner, orange juice commercial advocate, and fundamental Christian, was the stalwart voice against the county approving of such an abomination.

Jerry Falwell, from his perch in Lynchburg, Virginia, was cheering Anita on this crusade, which ultimately failed. The measure was rescinded, thanks to the efforts of Mrs. Bryant, which would have granted to gays equal housing and employment rights in the county. There was nothing wrong in what they sought in that regard. Ultimately, gay rights would win out, and ironically,

Anita Bryant's crusade helped to bring attention to it and advanced it, as pointed out in a 2007 *Sun Sentinel* article. I think exclusion of gay people from mainstream life was an ideology itself that was bound to fail in the light of fairness and reason.[90]

The 1980s then brought the crises of HIV and AIDS, which started out in the gay community but spread throughout the general population. The initial hostility of those who condemned the outbreak as a "gay disease" and "God's judgment on the gay community" became a point of solidarity and compassion, as the country pulled together to combat the illness and develop treatments.

Starting in the 1990s, gays could serve in the military in a "don't ask, don't tell" policy, and in recent years, they could serve openly. Celebrities came out and proudly so. Civil unions were recognized under insurance policies, and more recently, the Supreme Court approved gay marriage, as many states already had, even though some wondered about the ramifications of such an action for the traditional definition of marriage. There has also been a growing movement to discourage violence against the LGBT community, and laws have been passed to discourage discrimination and violence, otherwise known as "hate crimes."[91]

Yet the hidden agenda of some folks within this movement have changed into something increasingly disturbing, especially over the last twenty years. A group calling themselves LGBTQ now garners support and affirmation, and the rainbow, which had been a symbol of many lovely things, not the least of which was God's promise to never flood the earth again, has become a symbol of various sexual identities.

In Romans 1:21–24 (NIV), Paul offers a rather stern admonition about wanton sexual activity. The passage is placed in the context of God's wrath against the ungodly activities of the world:

> For although they knew God, they neither glorified him as God nor gave thanks to him, but their thinking became futile and their foolish hearts

were darkened. Although they claimed to be wise, they became fools and exchanged the glory of the immortal God for images made to look like a mortal human being and birds and animals and reptiles.

Therefore, God gave them over in the sinful desires of their hearts to sexual impurity for the degrading of their bodies with one another. They exchanged the truth about God for a lie and worshipped and served created things rather than the Creator, who is forever.

I prefer the way the King James puts it: they "worshipped the creature instead of the creator" (Romans 1:24 KJV). As the passage progresses, it speaks of unseemly sexual acts and other terrible traits. However, it should be noted that many NT scholars put this passage in the context of temple prostitution and orgies that Paul may have become familiar with in his encounter with the Greco-Roman world.

Paul would not have known about homosexuality as an orientation but as a sexual act, in the same way that incest or bestiality or intercourse with animals were sexual acts. I have come to understand that there appears to be legitimate psychological and biological issues that result in alternative sexual and gender orientations.

Quaker theologian Richard Foster, in his book *Money, Sex & Power*, described homosexuality as an expression of our sexual brokenness and said gay partnerships should be allowed on that basis. This is a very compassionate position. Foster was criticized by many for his pro-gay stance at the time his book came out several years ago. Yet today, Foster is deemed as intolerant by the current crop of LGBTQ advocates in and out of the mainline church, because he still upholds traditional heterosexual relationships as God's intended ideal.[92]

I do not believe that Paul was referring in Romans to someone like college freshmen who struggle with their sexual orientation. Instead, he spoke of homosexuality in the context of a general human wickedness and rebellion against God. The key to understanding the passage is in the phrase "worshipped the creature [or created things] instead of the creator."

Let's face it, the most seductive idols are not the imaginary ones but the ones that possess real power. Sex and money possess real power. It is why material and sexual hunger are the issues that are most often addressed in scripture, along with power, of course, although the other two idols dovetail very readily with that one.

Embedded in sex is the God-given power of creation. What could be more powerful than being able to create life? We are all here because of that power. What could be more powerful than the erotic allure of sexual desire and the powerful intimacy and satisfaction that comes with it?

The greatest plays, poetry, sonnets, stories, and music ever composed were about sex. The Song of Solomon in the Old Testament is a seductive and erotic love poem. Is there any product in America, or the globe, for that matter, where sex does not play a role in selling it? The advertising world of Madison Avenue is practically a cesspool of ideas for using sex to sell products, from cars to indoor plumbing. Politics, from ancient times to the present, revolve around sex, and power has been called by many the ultimate aphrodisiac.

Yet like all powers that God has unleashed in this world, how sex is expressed and channeled is critically important. It can create the experience of a couple being "one flesh," as Jesus describes it in the sexual consummation of marriage. It can "complement marriage," as a former pastor of mine in Florida once remarked, "in the creation of children."

However, the dark side of sexual expression has always been very much a part of the human experience. Sex can be a very destructive power. Prostitution, sexual slavery, and promiscuity are among the many destructive channels that sexual energy passes through, and in pornography, we see images of sex that relate it to power.

Pornography, a long-standing staple of erotic and sexual appetites, is one way that the worship of sex has been cultivated. "I am going to … this woman. I am going to … him all day long." Sex is not seen in this context as an expression of intimacy but of power and even violence. What is rape in the mind of a deranged person but the ultimate expression of power and violence against another person?

Sex transmits many diseases that have plagued humanity with illness, insanity, and death for millennia. As my father once remarked, "Promiscuity is an unsanitary activity." Syphilis, gonorrhea, and the AIDS epidemic are among the many diseases that have been spread through sexual intercourse of one form or another. These diseases indicate that the channels of sexual activity matter; God was not simply being prudish in warning against unbridled sexual activity. I don't even need to mention the unwanted pregnancies and abortions that promiscuous activity results in.

That brings me back to my original point: Have you noticed that with the LGBTQ community, equality is no longer the focus, as it was with actions like the 1977 referendum in Dade County? One hears the language of power as these groups demand that churches, businesses, and the society in general recognize not only their equality but also their political and social prominence.

A minister can hardly speak a word critical of the gay movement without being threatened with legal action by one group or another. Institutions of faith feel threatened in their hiring practices and in deciding what kind of weddings they will allow.

Mainline churches, wanting to be open and compassionate, are accommodating themselves to an agenda that is not necessarily compassionate or tolerant toward dissenting views. Certainly not toward those with a traditional sexual value system. The labeling of heterosexuals with terms like *cis-gender* or *heterosexism* are designations seething with overtones of social contempt, as I perceive them.

Interestingly enough, the founder of #Walkaway, an organization of people walking away from the Democratic party and the radical LGBTQ agenda, is a homosexual who could not fathom why hatred and contempt of heterosexuals had become a part of the LGBTQ agenda.[93]

The liberal mainline church, in the name of tolerance, is now accommodating itself to movements that appear to be intolerant toward anyone who would even raise a moral question about certain sexual agendas. The Salvation Army is the latest group this movement has sought to stigmatize. Academic institutions that pride themselves on their avant-garde advocacy undergird the attitudes of the mainline churches.

Am I one to argue that gays should have no place in the life of the world or the church? No, I am not. I think the hatefulness of many conservative Christian groups toward the gay community pushed our culture to this unfortunate place. This hatefulness reached its height with the mocking and disrespect showed by the Westboro Baptist Church from Kansas toward the homosexual community, by sending their members to protest at the funerals of gay soldiers and veterans, in order to dishonor their memory with signs spouting hateful epitaphs.

Imagine what was on those distasteful signs. The late Jerry Falwell even remarked, "Someone would have to be meaner than the devil to do that at someone's funeral." The late Fred Phelps, the pastor of the Westboro congregation, even had the audacity to protest Falwell's funeral because of the sentiments he expressed.[94]

Some in the LGBTQ community appear to be having their revenge on a traditional society that was hateful and even violent toward them, and understandably so. Many Christians, particularly straight ones, did not communicate much love to our gay brothers and sisters, and society is now paying for this. Traditional Christians, like gays today, forgot that when we use sex for power over others, we are in effect worshiping a created idol instead of the creator. We are all fallen creatures who should point our brothers and sisters to the One who redeems us all.

Now the idol of sex is being used to punish the traditional religious community. The current appropriation of sex is being used to influence the minds of young children and confusing them about their gender development. What is this but sacrificing the innocence of children to a god? It is an expression of sexual power being imposed upon children. Many are buying into this gender-fluid belief system without examining the potentially harmful psychology underlying it.

We have the appalling medical procedures of sexual reassignment being imposed upon children. Males fought for the right to compete in women's sports; how is that fair, considering the physical advantages that males generally have over females? This situation turns the whole idea of women's sports on its head. Yet who cares, since the distinction between males and females is imagined to be fluid, regardless of what science has established as fact or what God decreed in Creation?

Librarians are now backed into a corner by their own association, feeling like they have no choice but to welcome drag queens to read books to children.[95] Some in the transgender community think they have an inherent right to share the same public bathroom with women and little girls. I have personally thought that having public family or unisex bathrooms as a third option would be a good compromise, but that idea doesn't appear to suit the agenda.

The unfairness of all of this should be apparent to most people, since we are not talking about justice for all here but an effort to quell reasonable opposition to the overreach of a sexual agenda. Talk of God, unfortunately, is conspicuously absent from any of the debates about sex or gender roles. Our culture is worshipping at a different altar. The worship of sex present in the Greco-Roman world is now out of control in our own.

I find this very troubling as a Christian pilgrim and wish we could get back to a place where we uphold Christian sexual standards and gender roles and still be merciful and affirming. I sometimes fear that our society and church are both too late to repair the damage.

Some people say that Jesus never mentioned homosexuality, to suggest that he would not be bothered by it. I think this is an interesting but questionable conclusion. This kind of reasoning is called an argument from silence. I do not recall Jesus disputing the Levitical laws pertaining to sexual morality but expressing the sentiment of mercy in how such laws should be enforced. I do think he would have loved many of the gay people I have come to love, as he expressed love for so many others.

Finally, we are all sinners, and each of us has needed forgiveness for something. I like how this is expressed in 1 Corinthians:

> Or do you know that the unrighteous will not inherit the kingdom of God? Do not be deceived: neither the sexually immoral, nor idolaters, nor adulterers, nor men who practice homosexuality, nor thieves, nor the greedy, nor drunkards, nor revilers, nor swindlers, will inherit the kingdom of God.
>
> And such were some of you. But you were washed, you were sanctified, you were justified in the name of the Lord Jesus Christ and by the Spirit of our God. (1 Corinthians 6:7–11 ESV)

My concern about the LGBTQ agenda is not about whether we are called to love people for all of who they are. There are many good LGBTQ people. Many are people of faith I know, love, have worked with, and have acted alongside on stage. I could perform a gay wedding and feel content that God was pleased with my action. I have no problem with ministering in the LGBTQ community.

I have no pressing concern or fear about gays working in the church. I knew and implicitly trusted people who were gay members of my church growing up; they worked on our church staff.

The LGBTQ community has had its own home in the Metropolitan Church denomination for years and is now present in my old denomination and other mainline bodies. I have known gay people all my life and am hardly what could be termed homophobic. My involvement with the whole issue hits close to home for me, in more ways than I can share.

I do not live in a perfect Christian bubble, and I never have. My concerns are about the promotion of an ideology that has become increasingly militant in its demands on our society and institutions of faith. Not all LGBTQ people promote this kind of militancy, but it has become an agenda that some self-professed leaders of that community are using to hurt society, in my opinion, out of a sense of denied entitlement and deep injury.

In short, what this troubled Christian pilgrim has discovered is that people being gay, multisexual, or multigendered is not a spiritual problem for me. However, their insistence on setting up a sexual ideology as the god others must bow down to and worship is a problem for me. We should all submit to the living God who wants to make us all spiritually and sexually whole. I pray for the day love wins out over ideology.

Chapter 5

IS IT REAL OR VIRTUAL?

Connections in a Virtual World

It has been said that what our current generation needs is a sense of connection. In the country of Portugal, it was discovered that the most effective way to combat substance abuse was by helping addicts get jobs and reconnect with society. Some see this as a novel discovery. Yet biblical history is a testimony to the power of connection in bringing about spiritual, mental, and even physical health.[96]

Just a thought for the reader: Do you have a portable phone or like to spend time on a tablet, laptop, or desktop computer? Go on social media? Me too. I spend way too much time on Facebook. The lure of it is powerful. I have been on social media now for ten years.

Yet I have learned something in that time. The internet has real limitations in terms of connection. The sad irony of our times is that on a communication level, we have never been more connected as people and groups. Yet on a relationship level, many people have never felt less connected. That raises an important issue. Instead of making us feel more connected, the virtualness of the medium itself highlights the disconnection. How can the

Gospel address this? How can the Gospel address a world of a thousand virtual relationships? By highlighting the power of simply having a few actual relationships.

There is an epidemic of depression and despair in our society, which is related to a growing sense of isolation, despite an abundance of virtual relationships on social media, which gets to the important question that I would like to explore here. How can the Gospel bring real connection to the world? It's a good spiritual question now that we are entering the third decade of a century where our life has become so intrinsically related to technology.

A college professor in the greater New York area once asked me, "Robert, what do you think are the two most common remedial courses for college freshmen?"

"What courses?" I inquired.

"Writing and speaking," he said. He went on to explain to me that many young people believe that phone text shorthand is actual grammar, and verbal skills are often underdeveloped because so much conversation occurs in a virtual medium.

Well, that makes sense, considering how many high school students today peck on their phones to send texts to each other even when they are sitting next to each other. Our lives have indeed become increasingly immersed in this virtual world. Also, let's face it, for good or bad, the grammar that we use is the grammar that we know. Our speaking skills are developed through conversing.

Biblical history itself is about divine connections and conversations. God made a personal connection to Abram, who then became the father of a people. God calls individuals to himself. He called a leader named Moses, who in turn led a people. He even downloaded to Moses words to a tablet from a cloud (bad attempt at humor, folks).

Yet Moses himself related to only a few individuals, with whom he actually shared his life. His brother Aaron was a much better speaker than he was, his father-in-law Jethro advised him how to govern the people, and his military leader Joshua helped to lead the people through the wilderness and into the Promised Land. God does call a people, but in a way characterized by personal, vertical, and horizontal connection.

Jesus ministered to the multitudes, but he related himself to only twelve people. Kind of amazing when you consider that he was the Savior of the world. He spoke to crowds of thousands and understood the value of mass communication. However, he only personally associated with twelve men. There is something profound about that fact when you think about it.

There were many who needed to hear from him, who would benefit from his touch, his healing power, his counsel, but in the end, his most important ministry was investing himself in that twelve, and one of them would even be a very large disappointment. Jesus understood the importance of making real connections. We read in the Gospel of John:

> I've told you these things for a purpose: that my joy might be your joy, and your joy wholly mature. This is my command: Love one another the way I loved you. This is the very best way to love. Put your life on the line for your friends. You are my friends when you do things, I command you. I'm no longer calling you servants because servants don't understand what their master is thinking and planning. No, I've named you friends because I've let you in on everything I've heard from the Father. (John 15:11–15 MSG)

As an aside, the virtualness of social media has also led to something called cyberbullying. Children in school are often cruelly singled out, exploited, and attacked by others on social media. Some victims end up taking their own lives. Very tragic.

The anonymity of the medium fosters a mob mentality, reminding one of the cruel mob that called out for the Crucifixion of the Lord. Mobs can be brazened and unrestrained. As someone who has spent time on social media, I have seen how cruel people can be toward each other, because of the virtualness of the medium and the moblike anonymity that it provides. We are not hurting a real person we can imagine, or rationalize, just a phantom in a virtual world.

Yet none of us are phantoms, and the effects of such cruelty are not confined to the virtual world. A few years ago, there was even a story about a football player from Notre Dame Manti T'eo, who fell in love with a girl on social media, only to discover that the entire relationship had been well-orchestrated scam.[97]

Jesus was never a coward the way people can be in the virtual world. He called people hypocrites and vipers to their face, and it is because they deserved it. He also never criticized anyone without offering helpful and healing counsel along with it.

Yet as a leader and teacher, he related to his disciples in the most personal and kindest of ways. Rabbis or teachers typically called their students servants or slaves. It is in this context that Jesus said in John 15:15 (NLT), "I no longer call you servants, because a master doesn't confide in his slaves. Now you are my friends, since I have told you everything the father told me."

Relationships are vital. The personal relationships you have are vital. Those relationships are tangible and real. The Gospel itself is lived out in such tangible ways.

I had to take a hiatus from Facebook just so that I could finish this book. The mental energies that social media drains from us often far exceed any benefits we receive from it. However, if you are a social media person like me, you might consider cutting your time on it in half and invest more of it in the people you can physically spend time with. You could also choose a day where you take a sabbath or day of rest from social media. Have I been saying that our relationship with technology is altogether bad? No.

I say this especially to the younger readers: The one or two good friends you have a real relationship with are worth a hundred virtual ones. God created us for relationships and connection. Reconnecting to small but real groups of people is the antidote, I believe, to the illusory world of virtual relationships. Our new virtual reality does open us up to the world in amazing ways; it can be used to strengthen our tangible relationships and even establish others, but one thing I am certain of: It's not a substitute for the same.

We need tangible relationships for our spiritual, emotional, and psychological health. God created us to be in relationship with him and with others. I can tell you, as someone who has spent a good deal of my life being lonely, the few good relationships I've had sustained me in ways I cannot begin to explain.

Do I keep up with those relationships on Facebook? You bet I do, but those relationships were not forged there. God has hopefully blessed you with tangible relationships with people you feel a connection to. That is a blessing beyond words. That is a real-life investment. Continue to cultivate those investments, and don't allow the virtual world to impinge upon those vital personal relationships.

Ironically, as I finish this book, the coronavirus quarantine has many of us relying on communications technology more than ever before. We are having meetings online, conducting business online, and attending worship services online. I recently participated in a Good Friday service online. I am thankful that we have this technology.

However, have you noticed something? There is still a deep longing in this crisis, for people to connect in nonvirtual ways. Just recently, members of a church in Kentucky showed up for an outdoor service in their cars. The local police fined them five hundred dollars a car. The injustice of that action is not something I want to address here. Yet there are positives to this difficult situation. Families are spending more time together, and people are getting to know their neighbors, something that has been curbed by our mobile and constantly moving culture. People are also taking the time to think and reflect. Perhaps this would be a good time to consider how empty our lives have become, apart from the manic business we live in, something that we can do other than attend Zoom meetings and scour Facebook.

Like the time Jesus spent with the twelve disciples, the time you spend with your Christian friends, family, neighbors, and mentors is the time when you will make the most lasting impact on your life and their lives. Perhaps some of you younger readers can be those things to someone else in the future. Build real connections in this virtual world.

The Kingdom of God and the Fiefdoms of Humanity

Human beings are political animals, by and large. We engage in the world's politics out of our personal beliefs and out of our individual or group interests. This political engagement involves issues of law, governance, world affairs, and economics. Politics is the art of advocating for certain views, soliciting professional politicians and political parties, and advocating on our individual and group behalf.

Christians and others bring to bear their values in this arena, but it is a human arena. It is a human fiefdom. A *fiefdom* can be defined as an estate that is controlled by an economic and political leader, called a lord or noble. This come from feudalism, which was system in the Middle Ages of lands granted by a king in exchange for military service or some other favor. These lands would be lived on and cultivated by a dependent class of people called serfs and vassals.

Yet there is an ongoing debate in Christian circles over which feudal lords are faithful to Christ. I read a book by a Christian acquaintance from years past who argued that the political right was wrong and the political left reflected the Christian faith more deeply. As much as I respect this person, I think that it is a spiritual hazard to equate the platforms of any group with the Kingdom of God.

I begin my discussion with an observation made by Abraham Lincoln from his second Inaugural Address:

> Both read the same Bible and pray to the same God, and each invokes his aid against the other. It

may seem that any man should dare to ask a just God's assistance in wringing their bread from the sweat of other men's faces, but let us judge not, that we be not judged. The prayers of both could not be answered. That neither has been answered fully. The Almighty has his own purposes.

As Lincoln eloquently put it, "the almighty has his own purposes."[98] Back in 1979, Jerry Falwell organized a political movement called the Moral Majority. It was made up of a loose coalition of conservative Protestants, Catholics, Jews, and Mormons who were concerned about the precipitous moral decline of the country at that time. One can only wonder what the late Jerry Falwell would think of the current moral state. However, I digress. Many political pundits credit the Moral Majority and like-minded groups in helping to elect Ronald Reagan as president in 1980.

Yet this moral and political revival appeared to be short-lived, as business as usual in American politics resumed in the 1990s. Are we called to be salt and light in our culture and politics? Yes, I really think so. However, while we can seek to influence the fiefdoms of humanity with the Kingdom of God, the project of remaking such fiefdoms into the image of the kingdom is a project that will always ultimately fail.

At this point, you may imagine that I am a real stick in the mud and cynic who does not want to promote kingdom values in the world. Quite the contrary. For a long time, I was an unhappy cynic who really wanted to be an idealist. But after you've gotten beaten up in political conversations on Facebook and seen the end result of what your vote produces, then you can start to feel that the fiefdoms of humanity are always rigged to favor the political lords and nobles. Certainly not the vast number of serfs and vassals who are called upon to cast a ballot at the polls. Those of us who stand at the edge of power and influence can sometimes feel like our voices are mute.

In the 2016 presidential election, the serfs or "deplorables" chose Donald Trump, who the establishment lords found equally distasteful. How could a man who at times was engaged in questionable business practices and married three times be the leader who would help the nation's serfs or be amenable to the concerns of Christians?

You might still be wondering about that, as controversy surrounds his presidency. Yet for those of you who voted for Hillary Clinton or anyone else in the presidential election, God also loves you as well. However, God may show you something, if you are open to new insights; even as I write now, the opposition party continues to work to impeach and unseat him from his office. I know I personally did a lot of praying during the turbulent and ugly 2016 election, the Russian investigation, and the recent impeachment debacle.

Yet King Saul and David, both of whom were deeply flawed in similar ways to Trump, turned out to be the leaders God anointed for the people. We must remember, it was not God's idea for the people to have a king, but once it was decided that they wanted one, the prophet Samuel was called by God to anoint, pray for, and hold those leaders accountable. This is perhaps what has happened to Trump in November 2019, when the clergy came to Washington DC to pray for and with him. By inviting their counsel and prayers, he may yet lead the country out of its abyss, despite his personal flaws.[99]

Which means that our calling is not to create the Kingdom of God on earth but to pray and work for the presence of God's Kingdom, to break forth with power amid the human ones. God influenced nations of old that way. Our nation was born in prayer as well as in gunfire. The movement against slavery resulted from the prayers and actions of faithful people. The Civil Rights movement happened the same way. This is how a nation falling apart elected an unlikely politician like Abraham Lincoln. This is how a troubled nation came together in prayer during two devastating world wars and after the shocking attack on September 11, 2001.

After all, the kingdom breaking forth in power is what our Lord Jesus modelled, as the way its reality ultimately makes itself known to us. This power often breaks through when things look their most hopeless, but that's when we are more inclined to look to God for an answer.

As I worked to finish this book, I found myself in the middle of a national and global crisis, pertaining to the coronavirus or COVID-19. Our nation and its businesses, organizations, houses of worship, municipal agencies, and schools were shut down to contain the spread of a disease that originated in China and for which a vaccine has yet to be developed.

Yet I can see the Kingdom of God breaking forth in power, as many citizens are pulling together and getting on their knees to combat this common health menace. Unfortunately, just like in the past, it troubles me as a Christian pilgrim that some people are more concerned about exploiting such a situation politically than going to their knees in prayer for our citizens and our world.

However, as Lincoln said before, "the Almighty has his own purposes." Perhaps, God may well use this current crisis to help the people of this nation and of other nations to put things into perspective. Then many could start to realize that there are more important considerations in this world than just our selfish political or financial interests.

There are lives at stake and souls that are being confronted by their own mortality. The prospect of dying has a way of clarifying what is important. What is it that we want to leave behind in this world, and how do we want to be remembered? Did we stand up for what was right, despite hardships and opposition? Did we carry the cross of Christ, in the expectant hope that someday our witness will be applauded by our creator?

Hopefully, by the time you are reading my book, the outcome of this COVID-19 crisis, as well as its lasting meaning, will begin to emerge (or will be revealed by hindsight). That is something that both of us will discover as we travel down this portion of the river of history, as God unfolds his purpose before us.

As an aside, each of us, no matter what party we belong to, can model Christlike patience in our political and social discourses. As a veteran of social media, learning to be patient in that way has honestly been a struggle. However, I remind myself that just as I like to be heard, so do others. Listening is often even more important than speaking. Call it the golden rule as applied to conversation.

Whether we agree with someone else's opinions should not dictate if we treat them with kindness and respect. Jesus was also skilled at disarming caustic comments with a gentle response, and as Paul reminds us in Romans 12:20 (KJV), we are to "heap coals of fire" upon the heads of unkind people, by being kind to them, as a way of shaming bad behavior.

Lastly, none of us should have to take abuse, and sometimes, cutting off the conversation is the most Christian thing to do. Ultimately, God will judge them as he judges us. God's purpose is greater than the moment or issue at hand. We would do well to remember that.

Why Care about History?

Years ago, when I was in high school (and we are talking many years ago), my favorite teacher was a history teacher. Unlike many who teach history, my eleventh grade history instructor enjoyed his subject and was passionate about it. He once told me, "Robert, history is alive, and we are living in it." I have always loved history as well. My father had a habit of stopping at the roadside history signs during our vacation trips just to see what was so significant about a patch of ground. I would study history in college. I have a very historical consciousness.

So I trust you can understand why it bothers me that so many high school seniors cannot tell you when the moon landing was or even the year of Kennedy's assassination, which by the way coincides with the year I was born. I am disappointed that so many instructors in history fail to convey the passion about the subject of my high school history teacher.

After all, what is the Bible but the history of a people seen through the lens of faith? History is the realm of human activity and divine purpose. It is a like a river that carries us along from the past to the future. When we are born, we step into that river that came from before and behind us, and we are therefore touched and molded by what has gone on before. Flowing into the future, our lives touch those who are yet unborn. We were shaped by what came before and those who come after us will be shaped by what we are creating now.

History, therefore, is not merely the study of the past or memorizing boring dates and facts. It is the living river of human existence. In fact, what is the purpose of studying this chronicle of human existence? Is it not that we may learn from both the triumphs and tragedies of people who came before us?

As a young child, I would spend time talking with the elderly in the churches we attended. I learned a lot about living and dying from them. Just as important, I learned about what kind of world existed before I was born. I was able to appreciate what I had and put my own times in their proper perspective. I encourage my readers to spend time with older people. Get them to talk about themselves and their lives. They are living documents of history.

As a kid, I also loved reading biographies. In fact, my elementary school librarians insisted that I read at least some fiction because they were concerned that my reading preferences were too narrow. I can appreciate their concerns more now than I could then. However, there is a reason I loved biographies. They were the history of individuals, but not only the history of just any individuals, but ones who influenced our larger history. I found inspiration in reading about the stories of real people who had overcome real obstacles and challenges to do something special in the world.

I read about Benjamin Franklin, Benjamin Banneker, Thomas Edison, and Sir Isaac Newton. These, of course, were biographies written for children, but they helped to whet my appetite for mature biographies later. I have long believed that one of the keys to opening the minds and hearts of children is to have them read about great people. It is hard to expose yourself to the lives of truly exceptional people and not have their positive example influence your life and thinking.

I am troubled as a Christian pilgrim that for many children and young people, their role models and influences are selected for them by popular culture. While there are a few singers, rappers, and celebrities who rise to the bar of worthwhile people, their number is too meager to feel much encouragement about their influence. Although I have discovered that some in the rap field can rise to the occasion.

Kanye West may be the bridge that Christianity has needed to the next generation. I recently purchased the *Jesus Is King* CD, which was put together by rap music artist Kanye West. West is the rapper who recently found Jesus, and he's dedicating his music to the Lord. I never cared much for Kanye West; I thought he was a braggart. However, now I love Kanye West. I am a fan.

I never cared much for rap music, either, not only because of the style, but due to its degrading sexual and violent content. However, my adopted son enjoys listening to rap music in the car, and I allow him to do so at a low volume, even though the lyrics can make me cringe.

I played *Jesus Is King* in the car CD player this afternoon on the way to one of my son's appointments. The songs were a blessing, and we both enjoyed it. My son for the music style, and me for the messages that were presented. The songs are a compelling mix of rap, gospel, and blues. I think Kanye has helped me bridge a music generation gap with an uplifting message. God bless Kanye West.[100]

Still, children need guidance in terms of what they are consuming and digesting into their minds and souls. My elementary school librarians were not entirely wrong about that. I for one became a fan of *Encyclopedia Brown* mysteries. I developed at least a passing interest in fiction, and that was a good balance for me.

One of the problems in our current internet and virtual culture is the mistaken notion that access to knowledge leads to knowledge. This is a profound fallacy. What distinguishes an educated person from an uneducated one? Is it simply that they possess more general knowledge than the average person? Actually, no. It is that the educated person, presumably, understands what is worth knowing.

They can tell the difference between a diamond and a lump of coal. They can tell you why an understanding of Shakespeare is more important to Western culture than knowing what the Kardashians are wearing. They have been guided toward examples of the best thought and information in all disciplines of human learning. Unfortunately, I am troubled as an educated person and as a Christian humanist by the decline of our education, particularly in the areas of liberal arts.

It troubles me how public education has sought to dumb down arts, literature, and history rather than inspire the lives of children and young people. It troubles me that political agendas are being used to defame the ideas of Western culture, even at our Ivy League universities. Often this is done on the pretense that there is something inherently evil about Western culture or that other cultures should be studied. Frankly, on the surface, I see no problem with that. I have enjoyed studying about Eastern culture, religion, medicine, and literature.

However, let me ask the reader this: How can you compare the merits of Eastern and Western culture unless you have a good understanding of both? Education today is not in the business of opening minds, as I see it, but of closing them. Rather than opening the minds of young people to various sources of knowledge and inspiration, we are indoctrinating them into the tenets of group-think, driven by the agendas of political and social advocates. You might get good little foot soldiers for your pet causes this way, or young people who might vote a certain way to be sure, but let me ask you this: Is this how you get the next George Washington Carver, Albert Einstein, or Ralph Waldo Emerson? I doubt it.

We hear much about the value of vocational education these days. I support vocational education. Even my ministry training was partially vocational. My training in special needs has been vocational. I also agree that not everyone is suited for college or should expend the expense of attending one. We need good electricians, mechanics, technicians, plumbers, and so forth. These are honorable professions, and they pay decent money. I can also personally attest to what it's like to be a liberal arts graduate and barely eke out a living.

So what is it that troubles me? What troubles me is that we have forgotten the value of education for its own sake, for the sake of enriching our humanity and being able to pass on the legacy of centuries of wisdom and knowledge to the next generation.

Okay, Socrates was a chauvinist. So what? Spit out the bone, like they used to say, and enjoy the value of the fish. Besides, it is arrogant to evaluate people from the past by our own standards. How well will our thoughts and actions fare a hundred years from now? Would we want to be judged by the standards of another time or on the merits of our thoughts in the time in which we lived? Understanding the context of knowledge is, after all, also a sign of an educated person.

Chapter 6

DISAPPOINTMENT WITH GOD

The last words of Jesus on the cross was a quotation from Psalm 22:2 (NIV): "My God, my God, why have you forsaken me?" The Psalms, as a matter of fact, are filled with pleadings of disappointment with God. If you have not read the book of Psalms or haven't read them in a while, I suggest you reacquaint yourself with them. It is an eye-opening read. So is the book of Job, where God allows Satan to destroy this man's existence, just short of taking his life.

Job's wife summarizes how many of us would look at such a situation: "His wife said to him, 'Why do you still trust God? Why don't you curse him and die?'" (Job 2:9 CEV).

I often say that it's okay to be angry with God. First, because he has large enough shoulders to endure our anger. Second, because it is a way of relating to God as a real and tangible person. Don't we get mad at our parents, our siblings, our children, our friends, and our government? It is not a lack of faith in their reality that spurs on our anger but our assurance that these people and institutions are very real. When we get angry with God, it is an act of faith. We are acknowledging that there is someone there to be angry at. Finally, God is not indifferent to the human situation, and this gets to the core of my point.

However, before I get to that point, I would like to discuss prayer for a moment. We live in a time when many are rediscovering the power of prayer, and I am glad to see that happening. However, faith can sometimes be used to injure wounded people, like Job's comforters who kept insisting that bad fortune had befallen him because he was either unfaithful to God or had failed to exercise proper faith, both of which turned out to be false.

I really encourage you to read the book of Job. I would warn you that it's not a casual read and may require more than one sitting to get through. However, it has the deepest theological reflections to be found in the Old Testament and the entire Bible, for that matter. That is not just my opinion, but the perspective of the most eminent biblical theologians, modern and ancient. It is also thought by some to be the oldest book in the Bible to boot, which is remarkable.[101]

There are many who believe that God will do everything to spare his most beloved and faithful children of any difficulties, much less tragedy. That is a terrible misreading of the Bible; yes, sometimes prophets and apostles were spared from murder and disease. I know when my father was suffering from a brain tumor, we were praying for him, our church was praying for him, someone even called television evangelist and faith healer Benny Hinn to pray for him. My father did rally for a while during cobalt radiation treatments, and I had an opportunity to reconcile with him after a couple of years of estrangement. My dad encouraged me in the last few days of his life and shared with me how I should not hide my light under a bushel. I do see those things as an answer to prayer. However, in the end, he died at the age of sixty-six.

Recently, a person I worked with in special needs ministry had a teenage son who died in a freak car accident. He was an incredibly special and endearing young man. Many prayers, including my own, went up for this young man, but in the end, he died from his brain and body trauma. Many prayers have been offered up for those stricken by the coronavirus, and yet in the end, many of them have died as well.

Yet here I am, having written a book as a devout Christian still believing in Christ. So, what is my point? I remember back to my days in seminary; as I shared earlier, sometimes a professor would say something worth remembering. In this case, it was something that was shared in a course I took in New Testament theology.

We were having a discussion one day in class about the power of prayer, and my instructor remarked, "The most powerful faith in the world is not the faith that produces the miracles, but the faith that remains intact when the miracles do not occur." In other words, a faith that remains steadfast in believing in the goodness of God, even when the evidence for that goodness is not forthcoming. A faith that can weather loss, difficulties, and tragedy, and remain steadfast in loving and believing in God.

A minister named Dr. Harold Wilke was an occasional visitor to my home church in South Florida. He had been born without arms. Yet he did practically everything with his legs and feet that most of us do with our arms and hands. His watch band was on his leg. His van was rigged so he could drive it with his legs, feet, and mouth. He was also a major figure in getting Congress to pass the famous Americans with Disabilities Act; he was present when it was signed by President George H. W. Bush in 1990. Dr. Wilke died on February 25, 2003. He was eighty-eight.[102]

Dr. Wilke once gave a speech in which he recalled an incident when someone asked that if he had enough faith, would God grow back his arms? He replied, "If that person had enough faith, it could have the same result." Why did Dr. Wilke have no arms? Why did Paul have the thorn in his flesh? These are questions wrapped in a mystery, but as the Lord said to Paul, "My grace is sufficient for you" (2 Corinthians 12:9 NIV). Real faith, and real prayer, is not about the changes that God can bring to a situation, but about the internal changes that God can bring about in us, in terms of using our circumstances to his glory.

Certainly, Christ was glorified in the inspiring example of Dr. Wilke and his advocacy for those with disabilities. It can also be said that those who endure tragedy and still remain faithful to

Christ are much more inspiring examples than those who have experienced miracles (and let's face it, the latter can sometimes be insufferable in bragging about it). One person may humbly acknowledge God's power, but other people may use an answer to prayer to boast about their faith in a way that seeks to put others in a bad light.

Am I saying that I dismiss miracles? No, I very much believe in miracles and God's power. I have seen God's power at work. I pray for others and continue to ask for prayers. Yet I am reluctant to make my faith about miracles, as if God must tangibly prove himself to me before I am willing to believe in him. As I recall, wasn't that a temptation Satan presented to Jesus? Jesus responded that it was wrong to test God that way and expect him to perform miracles just for our satisfaction. That is hardly faith at all, but my objection as a troubled Christian pilgrim to some of the emphasis upon miracles goes even deeper.

When I was a ministry student, I did an internship on the geriatric floor of a hospital. I reported to an ordained Presbyterian chaplain, who had me write verbatim reports of my various visits. After he read one report, he strongly admonished me. I had visited with a woman who was going to have to surgically lose her legs, a very traumatic prospect. I recall saying something glib, like, "It's going to be all right. It is in God's hands." The chaplain scolded me that it was beyond my power to make a promise like that. He further clarified his point by sharing "that as ministers of the Gospel, the only promise we can confidently make is about the promise of the resurrection." Our ultimate hope is not in this life, but in the life to come. That is where we bring the most comfort.

That point was brought home to me even more strongly by a patient I visited on the geriatrics ward. He said, "Young man, as a minister of Christ, you bring the best news of anybody. Why do I say that? Because, whether we are talking about doctors, insurance people, or attorneys, the good news they bring me all ends at the grave. Whereas, young man, the good news you bring begins after the grave has happened."

As a troubled Christian pilgrim, in and out of the seminary classroom, we hear people bemoaning why God allows certain things to happen. There is a whole realm of theology committed to this question, called theodicy, an attempt to reconcile suffering and evil with the existence of a good God. Is God good but simply limited in what he can do, or is he not so good and does he not care as much as we believe? This question also raises the issue of how God governs our life circumstances, and the controversy concerning free will figures into it as well.

However, as useful as such exercises may be, I think those perspectives miss the most pressing point. The question for many is not "Why, God?" but "Where is God?" This, in fact, was the question Jesus posed from Psalms when he was on the cross: "My God, my God, why have you forsaken me?" (Psalm 22:2 NIV). In other words, where are you, God? I happen to believe that the abandonment that Christ felt was real. Part of the atonement Jesus made on the cross was to experience the separation from God that human beings experience when we feel abandoned by the Lord.

I have counseled people going through the stages of dying. I once served as an on-call minister at a hospital in South Florida. On one such call, a man requested that I read Isaiah to him. He had not been a faithful church member, by his own admission, but he wanted to make his peace with Christ. I read him the passage that he requested, and the very next day, this gentleman died.

What I have discovered is that when people are getting ready to take their last breath, their most pressing concern is whether there is something on the other side of the dark tunnel. Some may make fun of the pie-in-the-sky talk of Christians, but not those facing death. The existence of a life beyond death is, for them, the only question that matters.

If you read the book of Job, you will see at the end, all that he lost was restored. However, it has been argued that the restoration was a way of offering Job a somewhat happy ending after a tragic drama in the book. The ending is a bit too convenient, given the deep questions raised by the book, in my opinion. I don't think Job's losses could ever be adequately recompensed by God.

However, Job's perspective is not the only one that matters. In fact, when Job questions God, the Lord retorted, "Where were you when I laid the foundations of the earth?" (Job 38:4 ESV). A divine put-down, to be sure, but also a profound point. God's perspective on our life and all of existence is larger than ours. Yet despite everything Job has gone through, he does remain faithful to God, to the point of saying, "Though he slay me, yet will I hope in him" (Job 13:15 NIV), and "I know that my redeemer lives, and that in the end he will stand on the earth" (Job 19:25 NIV).

I do think that the book of Job is worth reading. However, the questions it poses are never adequately answered, as I see it. However, I think they were, in fact, answered in the most profound way possible in the incarnation of God coming to us as Jesus. In Jesus, God assumes the role of Job and more. Jesus was God coming down to us and standing on the earth as our redeemer. He becomes the one who is unfairly judged by his brethren; he is also persecuted by Satan and voluntarily takes the step that God even protected Job from, and that was the willing sacrifice of his own life. God answers the question of suffering by entering it and redeeming its meaning by being the One who redeems it.

What is the cross but the symbol of a suffering God, a symbol of a God who suffered for us and who suffers with us? The cross itself could be pictured like a road intersection, an intersection between our suffering and God's compassionate presence. Jesus is the one who is with us in the deepest moments of fear, grief, and loss. He can understand this because he intimately connected himself to those realities; therefore, we can count on God's empathetic humanity to bring us comfort in every situation. In the last judgment in Matthew 25:31–46, we are told where Jesus would be found: in the broken places, the places of tragedy, hunger, and imprisonment, the places where we might think God abandoned people, but truthfully, where God is the most intently present with them.

In scripture, God discloses to us a framework for understanding how he is present in the world and in our lives. Before we are inclined to give up hope and faith, let us look to that framework and evaluate God's presence in the light of it. We might be surprised to discover that he is there to offer us, as Paul described in Philippians 4:7 (NLT), "the peace of God that surpasses all understanding."

Afterword

I would like to thank my wife in helping me to develop the book, my counselor friend for his helpful feedback, Eric Schroeder in encouraging me to publish with Westbow Press, and its staff for managing the formatting and production of the book. The staff feedback was invaluable in helping me to keep this project on track for publication.

Lastly, I want to dedicate my book to my parents and family, who shaped my life journey and faith. I would also like to dedicate my book to my mentors, some of whom were mentioned in my book, who uplifted my heart and sharpened my mind.

Congratulations for reading through my book. The time you spent in digesting my thoughts is deeply appreciated. If you disagreed with some (or all) of my points, that is fine. I did not write this book to try to change the mind of anyone whose convictions were settled. I did write it to provide food for thought, to start a discussion on important issues, and to bring comfort to those troubled souls who might be sitting on the fence, wondering where their feet could land.

If my book has offered that place for you or someone else, then my purpose for writing it has been fulfilled. The Christian life is a journey or pilgrimage, and we grow and change over time. I trust that I have provided food for your soul and some encouragement for the next leg of your journey. In the words of Paul: "Being confident of this, he who began a good work in you, will carry it on to completion until the day of Christ Jesus" (Philippians 1:6 NIV).

Recommended Readings

Arakaki, R. *Constantine: The Great: Roman Emperor, Christian Saint, History's Turning Point*. Antiochian Orthodox Christian Archdiocese of North America, 2018. Retrieved from http://ww1.antiochian.org

Bloesch, D. G. Whatever Became of Neo-Orthodoxy? *Christianity Today*. December 1974. Retrieved from https://www.christianitytoday.com

Bustraan R. A. *The Jesus People Movement: A Story of Spiritual Revolution among the Hippies*. Eugene, OR: Pickwick Publications, 2014.

Cooper, B. "Is the Devil Real?" *exploreGod*, 2019. Retrieved from https://www.exploregod.com

D'Souza, D. *Falwell before the Millennium: A Critical Biography*. Regnery Gateway Publisher, 1984.

Elliot, Michael. *Playing Hide & Seek: A Non-Churchgoer's Path to Finding God*. Macon, GA: Smyth & Helwys Publishers, 1996.

Fox, F. H., and G. E. Morris. *Faith-Sharing: Dynamic Christian Witness by Invitation*. 1986. Retrieved from https://books.google.com/books

Fundamentalism. *United States History.* 2019. Retrieved from https://www.u-s-history.com

Gender Inclusive Language. *Chicago Divinity School of the Pacific.* 2019. Retrieved from https://cdsp.edu

Gonzalez, G., and J. W. Richards. *The Privileged Planet.* Washington DC: Regnery Publishing, 2015.

Hutchinson, R. J. "The Jesus Seminar Unmasked." *Christianity Today.* April 1996. Retrieved from https://www.christianitytoday.com

Macdonald, G. *All Shall Be Well: Explorations in Universal Salvation and Christian Theology, from Origen to Moltmann.* 2011. Retrieved from https://www.jstor.org/stable

Menninger, K. *Whatever Became of Sin?* Hawthorn Books, 1975.

Reisinger, J. G. *Total Depravity.* Frederick, MD: New Covenant Media, 2000.

Sproul, R. C. *What Is Reformed Theology: Understanding the Basics.* Grand Rapids, MI: Baker Books, 1997.

Strachan, O. *Awakening the Evangelical Mind.* Grand Rapids, MI: Zondervan, 2015.

Strauss, M. L., and D. Wegener. "The Inclusive Language Debate." Christian Research Institute, June 2009. Retrieved from https://www.equip.org

"The Self-Emptying of Christ." Fuller Seminary, 2019. Retrieved from https://www.fuller.edu

Warfield, B. B. *Studies in Tertullian and Augustine.* Greenwood Press, 1930.

Willimon, W. H. *Shaped by the Bible.* Nashville: Abingdon Press, 1990.

Wright, N. T. *Surprised by Hope: Rethinking Heaven, the Resurrection, and the Mission of the Church.* New York: Harper Collins Publishers, 2008.

Wynkoop, M. B. *Foundations of Wesleyan-Arminian Theology.* Beacon Hill Press, 1967.

Endnotes

1   Thomas A. Schafer, "Johnathon Edwards: American Theologian" (Encyclopedia Britannica, 2020), https://www.britannica.com

2   Justin Taylor, "85 Years Ago Today J.R.R. Tolkien Convinces C.S. Lewis That Christ Is the True Myth," *The Gospel Coalition* (September 20, 2016), https://www.thegospelcoalition.org

3   P. Janelle, "Muslims Converting to Christianity in Unprecedented Numbers Part I," *Open Doors* (June 28, 2017), https://www.opendoorsusa.org

4   Ron Hutchcraft, "Heroes of the Christian Faith: Edward Kimball," *Gospel Life* (May 16, 2016), http://www.gospel-life.net

5   Msgr. M. Francis Mannion, "Can I Walk to Emmaus?" *Our Sunday Visitor: For Catholics Who Love Their Faith* (2008), https://www.osvnews.com

6   Jeff McSwain, *Simul Sanctification: Barth's Hidden Vision for Human Transformation* (Eugene OR: Pickwick Publications, 2018), 110.

7   Valentyn Svit, "20 Methods of Evangelism: That Every Christian Should know," *Dude Disciple* (July 2, 2019), https://dudedisciple.com.

8   Fairchild, Mary. "Calvinism vs. Arminianism." Learn Religions. https://www.learnreligions.com/calvinism-vs-arminianism-700526 (accessed March 5, 2020).

9   Maud Newton, "Oy Vey Christian Soldiers," *The New York Times Magazine* (May 24, 2013): 48, https://www.nytimes.com.

10 U. M. Jeremy, "From Exclusivism to Universalism," *Hijacking Christianity* (March 16, 2011), http://hackingchristianity.net

11 K. A. Lawton, "More Ferment among Southern Baptists: Two Seminary Officials Tend Their Resignations, and the Washington Office Is Put on Notice." *Christianity Today* (November 20, 1987), https://www.christianitytoday.com

12 "Universalism and Horace Ballou," *Encyclopedia Britannica*, https://www.britannica.com/topic/Universalism

13   Kenneth Gullett, *A Firm Foundation* (Berlin: Verlag GD Publishing Ltd., 2017), 52–62.

14   E. Yamauchi, "Gnosticism," *The New International Dictionary of the Christian Church: Revised Edition*, ed. J. D. Douglas, Earle E. Cairns, and James E. Ruark (Grand Rapids, MI: Zondervan Publishing House, 1978), 417.

15   R. E. Nixon, "Resurrection of Christ," *The New International Dictionary*, 839.

16   Jeff Jensen, "Superman as Jesus—Christian Imagery in the Man of Steel," *Entertainment* (June 17, 2013), https://ew.com

17   Ralph P. Martin, "Kenosis," *The New International Dictionary*, 563.

18   Samuel J. Mikolaski, "Christology," *The New International Dictionary*, 223-224.

19   Carlos Levy, "Philo of Alexandria," *The Stanford Encyclopedia of Philosophy*, ed. Edward N. Zalta (2018), https://plato.stanford.edu/

20   Ed Eduljee, "The Buck Stops Here," Heritage Institute (2019), http://www.heritageinstitute.com.

21   Justin Taylor, "85 Years Ago Today," *The Gospel Coalition*, https://www.thegospelcoalition.org.

22   Larry Eskridge, "'Jesus People': A Movement Born from the 'Summer of Love'," *The Conversation* (September 15, 2017), http://theconversation.com.

23   Thomas Forsyth Torrance, "Karl Barth: Swiss Theologian," *Encyclopedia Britannica* (2020), https://www.britannica.com

24   John A. Battle, "Charles Hodge, Inspiration, Textual Criticism, and the Princeton Doctrine of Scripture," *WRS Journal* 4/2 (1997): 28–41, http://wrs.edu.

25   Mark Woods, "What Is the Chicago Statement on Biblical Inerrancy, and Why Should Evangelicals Believe It?" *Christianity Today* (March 2, 2018), https://www.christiantoday.com.

26   Robert H. Krapohl, "The Life of Carl Henry," *Henry Center for Theological Studies*, https://henrycenter.tiu.edu.

27   Cathy Cash, "Graham Urges Southern Baptists to Love Each Other," *UPI* (1988), https://www.upi.com.

28   Greg Koukl, "The Jesus Seminar under Fire," *Stand to Reason* (2016), https://www.str.org.

29   John Dart, "Seminar Rules Out 80% of Words Attributed to Jesus: Provocative Meeting of Biblical Scholars Ends Six Years of Voting

on Authenticity in the Gospels," *Los Angeles Times* (March 4, 1991), https://www.latimes.com.

30 Luke Timothy Johnson, "The Jesus Controversy: Why Historical Scholarship Cannot Find the Living Jesus," *America: The Jesuit Review* (August 2, 2010), https://www.americamagazine.org.

31 "To BCE or Not To BC? Common Era of BC and AD Appears to Be Over," *The Telegraph* (October 1, 2017), https://www.telegraph.co.uk.

32 Byron Borger, "William Willimon: Resident Alien," *Hearts & Minds* (1998), https://www.heartsandmindsbooks.com.

33 Dale H. Kuiper, "The Bible, a Divine Book: John Calvin's Doctrine of Holy Scripture," *Protestant Reformed Churches in America: Official Website* (1993), http://www.prca.org.

34 Bruce Hindmarsh, "What Is Evangelicalism," *Christianity Today* (March 14, 2018), https://www.christianitytoday.com.

35 Dr. Jill Carroll, "Protestantism, Eastern Orthodoxy & Catholicism," *World Religions, Professor.com* (2018), https://www.world-religions-professor.com

36 Fairchild, Mary. "The Apostles' Creed." Learn Religions (February 11, 2020), learnreligions.com/the-apostles-creed-p2-700364.

37 Justin Holcomb, "The Five Solas: Points from the Past that Should Matter to You," *Christianity.com* (July 13, 2012), https://www.christianity.com

38 Kevin Lawson, "Baptism, Communion, and Confirmation in the Reformation Movement: Impact on Ministry with Children in Churches Today, Part I," *The Book Blog: Talbot School of Theology* (2018), https://www.biola.edu.

39 Veronica Neffinger, "10 Things Everyone Should Know about Jehovah's Witnesses and Their Beliefs," *Christianity.com* (2020), https://www.christianity.com.

40 Albert C Outler, "Wesleyan Quadrilateral," *Theopedia* (2020), https://www.theopedia.com.

41 "John Huss: Christian History," *Christianity Today* (2020), https://www.christianitytoday.com.

42 Timothy George, "The Priesthood of All Believers," *First Things* (2020), https://www.firstthings.com.

43 Donald W. Dayton, "The Holiness and Pentecostal Churches: Emerging from Cultural Isolation," *Religion Online: Reprint of Christian Century article from 1979* (2020), https://www.religion-online.org.

44 Brannon Deibert, "Churches of Christ: 10 Things to Know about Their History and Beliefs," *Christianity.com* (2020), https://www.christianity.com.

45 Rod Janzen, "Old Order Christianity in the Central Valley: Old German Baptist Brethren, Holdeman Mennonites, and Spiritual Jumper Molokans," *Direction: A Mennonite Brethren Forum* 46, no. 4 (2017): 81–99, https://directionjournal.org.

46 Richard T. Vann, "Society of Friends: Religion," *Encyclopedia Britannica* (2020), https://www.britannica.com.

47 Susan Roach, "'You Gotta Go Crazy before You Can Be a Minister': Assessing a Speaking Role in the Primitive Baptist Church," *Folklife in Louisiana* (2019), http://www.louisianafolklife.org.

48 Doug Banwart, "Jerry Falwell, the Rise of the Moral Majority, and the 1980 Election," *Western Illinois Historical Review* Vol. 5 (2013): 133–56, http://www.wiu.edu.

49 "About Jan Linn," *Linnposts: Thinking against the Grain: Honest Talk about Religion, Politics & Social Issues* (2020), https://linnposts.com.

50 Darrell Laurant, "When the Civil War Came to Lynchburg," *The News & Advance* (June 15, 2014), https://www.newsadvance.com.

51 "Robert E. Lee Surrenders," *History.com, ed.* History.com editors (2020), https://www.history.com.

52 "Jimmy Carter Latest in Long Line of Presidents, Political Leaders to Visit LU," *Liberty University News Service* (May 17, 2018), http://www.liberty.edu.

53 Walter Unger, "Earnestly Contending for the Faith: The Role of the Niagara Bible Conference in the Emergence of American Fundamentalism 1875–1900," *Simon Fraser University: National Library of Canada* (1981): 118–54.

54 "Christian Fundamentalism," *Encyclopedia Britannica* (2020), https://www.britannica.com.

55 Melissa Petruzello, "Council of Jerusalem," *Encyclopedia Britannica* (2020), https://www.britannica.com.

56 "Martin Luther Defiant at Diet of Worms," *History.com*, ed. History.com editors (2020), https://www.history.com/

57 Rev. FR. George D. Konstantopoulos, "Saint Constantine and Helen," *Saint Andrew Greek Orthodox Church* (2016), http://saintandrewgoc.org/home.

58 Martin E. Marty and Francis Christopher Oakley, "Roman Catholicism," *Encyclopedia Britannica* (2020), https://www.britannica.com.

59 Melissa Petruzello, "Council of Chalcedon," *Encyclopedia Britannica* (2020), https://www.britannica.com

60 Sari Gilbert, "Pope Visits Lutheran Church," *The Washington Post* (December 12, 1983), https://www.washingtonpost.com

61 Armando Salguero, "Unrepentant Hypocrite Kaepernick Defends Fidel Castro," *The Miami Herald* (November 25, 2016), https://www.miamiherald.com

62 Joshua Prager, "Norma McCorvey: The Woman Who Became 'Roe'" then Regretted It," *Politico Magazine* (December 28, 2017), https://www.politico.com/magazine

63 Mary Farrow, "Did Thousands of Women Die from Illegal Abortions before Roe v. Wade? WaPo says No," *National Catholic Register* (December 14, 2019), https://www.ncregister.com/

64 Jessica Wakeman, "The Debate over Terminating Down Syndrome Pregnancies," *healthline* (August 29, 2017), https://www.healthline.com/

65 Cheryl K. Chumley, "Cannibalism: Scientist Says Eating Humans Could Save Earth," *The Washington Post* (September 6, 2019), https://www.washingtontimes.com/

66 Steve Ertelt, "Nine States Now Allow Killing Babies Up to Birth after Illinois Legalized All Abortions," *CatholicCitizens.org* (June 16, 2019), https://catholiccitizens.org/

67 Olufemi Terry, "China's Woman Shortage Creates an International Problem," *Share America* (September 30, 2019), https://share.america.gov/

68 Arthur Goldberg, "Abortion's Devastating Impact upon Black Americans," *Public Discourse* (February 11, 2019), https://www.thepublicdiscourse.com.

69 Nicole Fisher, "Science Says: Religion Is Good for Your Health," *Forbes* (March 29, 2019), https://www.forbes.com/

70 Greg Lanier, "No, 'Saul the Persecutor' Did Not Become Paul the Apostle," *The Gospel Coalition* (May 3, 2017), https://www.thegospelcoalition.org/

71 Erik Raymond, "Why Did Saul Change His Name to Saul?" *The Gospel Coalition* (March 14, 2014), https://www.thegospelcoalition.org/

72 Solomon Schechter and Wilhelm Bacher, "Gamaliel I," *Jewish Encyclopedia* (2011), http://www.jewishencyclopedia.com/

73 William A. Simons, "John the Baptist," *Bible Study Tools* (2020), https://www.biblestudytools.com/

74 Yoko Watasuki and James Griffiths, "Japan's Youth Suicide Rate Highest in 30 Years," CNN.com (November 6, 2018), https://www.cnn.com/

75 Hillary Hoffower, "70% of Millennials Say They'd Vote for a Socialist. 5 Facts about Their Debt-Saddled Economic Situation Tell You Why," *Business Insider* (November 1, 2019), https://www.businessinsider.com/

76 Stephen Hand, "Dickens v. Marx," *In the Alternative* (2017), https://stephenhand2012.wordpress.com/

77 Charles Dickens, "A Tale of Two Cities," *Goodreads* (2020), https://www.goodreads.com/

78 Anthony Gottlieb, "Atheists with an Attitude: Why Do They Hate Him?" *The New Yorker* (May 14, 2007), https://www.newyorker.com/

79 Ernie Tretkoff, "Heisenberg's Uncertainty Principle," *APS News* (2008), https://www.aps.org/

80 Del Ratzsch and Jeffrey Koperski, "Teleological Arguments for God's Existence," *Stanford Encyclopedia of Philosophy* (2005), https://plato.stanford.edu/

81 Erich Von Daniken, *Chariots of the Gods* (2020): http://www.daniken.com/

82 Lee Elliot Major, "Big Enough to Bury Darwin," *The Guardian* (August 23, 2001), https://www.theguardian.com/

83 Sir Fredrich Hoyle, *Quote Tab* (2019), https://www.quotetab.com.

84 Elizabeth Howell, "Fermi Paradox: Where Are the Aliens?" *Space.com* (April 27, 2018), https://www.space.com

85 Francis Collins, "The Language of God: A Scientist Presents Evidence for Belief," *BIOLOGOS* (2006), https://biologos.org/

86 Phillip Johnson, "Defending Intelligent Design," *NOVA: PBS* (September 30, 2007), https://www.pbs.org/

87 Mark L. Strauss and David Wegener, "The Inclusive Language Debate," *Christian Research Institute* (2009), https://www.equip.org/

88 Helen Pluckrose and James A. Lindsay, "Identity Politics Does Not Continue the Work of the Civil Rights Movements," *Areo* (September 25, 2018), https://areomagazine.com/.

89 "15 Famous Black Scientists in History," *Famous Scientists: The Art of Genius* (2020), https://www.famousscientists.org/

90 John Tanasychuk, "How Anita Bryant Fought—and Helped—Gay Rights," *Sun-Sentinel* (June 4, 2007), https://www.sun-sentinel.com/

91 "Milestones in the American Gay Rights Movement," *PBS American Experience* (2020), https://www.pbs.org.

92 Brantley W. Gasaway, *Evangelicals and the Pursuit of Social Justice* (New York: Oxford University Press, 2013), 177–78.

93 Jennifer Harper, "'WalkAway Campaign' Rejects Democratic Party, Plans 'Unsilent Majority March' on Washington," *The Washington Times* (January 15, 2020), https://www.washingtontimes.com/

94 Steven Nelson, "Westboro Baptist Church: Fred Phelps 'Has Gone the Way of All Flesh,'" *US News & World Report* (March 20, 2014), https://www.usnews.com/

95 Robert Knight, "'Drag Queen Story Hour' Shows What Has Gone Wrong in America," *The Washington Times* (October 11, 2019), https://www.washingtontimes.com/

96 Susan Ferreira, "Portugal's Radical Drug Policy Is Working, Why Hasn't the World Copied It?" *The Guardian* (December 5, 2017), https://www.theguardian.com/

97 Matt Gutman and Seni Tienabeso, "Timeline of T'eo Girlfriend Hoax Story," *ABC News* (January 21, 2013), https://abcnews.go.com/

98 Terrance Klein, "The Almighty Has His Own Purposes," *America: The Jesuit Review* (2013), https://www.americamagazine.org/

99 Marty Johnson, "Faith Leaders Pray for Trump at the White House," *The Hill* (November 1, 2019), https://thehill.com/

100 Andrew Chow, "How Kanye West's Controversial 'Jesus Is King' Is Dividing the Christian Community," *Time* (November 1, 2019), https://time.com/

101 Stephanie Hertzenberg, "What Is the Oldest Book in the Bible?," *beliefnet* (2020), https://www.beliefnet.com/

102 "Rev. Harold H. Wilke, 88," *Chicago Tribune,* reprint from the *Los Angeles Times* (March 4, 2003), https://www.chicagotribune.com/

Printed in the United States
By Bookmasters